LIFTING THE BLINDFOLD

Dr Alan Wood

ISBN-13:978-14699895 70
ISBN-10:14699895 73

Cover design by Izhar ul Haq

Printed in the United States of America

info@clearthinkingclearprofit.com

Grateful Acknowledgements

Sincere thanks to:

Anne and Charlie Kreitzberg
(www.agilecriticalthinking.com) for permission to re-work their Business Case for Critical Thinking as a key part of this book's introductory section

Daily Mail (http://www.dailymail.co.uk) for permission to use the article to illustrate complex correlations: www.dailymail.co.uk/news/article-2033796/Give-birth-March-pilot-August-bricklayer-December-dentist-.html

Don Shenker, Chief Executive Officer, **Alcohol Concern** (www.alcoholconcern.org.uk), for permission to use the charity's report "One on Every Corner" to illustrate the workings of correlation

Great Courses (www.thegreatcourses.com) for permission to adapt and expand concepts originally presented in: Zarefsky, David. "Underlying Assumptions of Argumentation (Lecture 2)" Argumentation: The Study of Effective Reasoning. DVD. Chantilly, VA: The Great Courses, 2006.

Independent (www.independent.co.uk) for permission to use the article by Steve Connor to illustrate visual impressions: www.independent.co.uk/travel/news-and-advice/the-real-danger-to-air-passengers-is-not-the-ash-cloud-andash-its-these-men-2289097.html

Sage Publications Ltd (www.sagepub.co.uk**)** for permission to adapt text from: Hutton, R and Hutton, G (2008) Passing Oxbridge Admissions Tests. Exeter: Learning Matters Ltd (www.learningmatters.co.uk)
And all my family and friends who shared the pain and the coffee as the book took shape

Of course, despite all the generous outside help that I have received, the responsibility for all errors remains mine.....

*"The world we have created is a product of our thinking:
it cannot be changed without changing our thinking."*
Albert Einstein

*"Nothing has such power to broaden the mind as the
ability to investigate systematically and truly all that
comes under thy observation in life."*
Marcus Aurelius

"Be gentle to all and stern with yourself."
Saint Teresa of Avila

LIFTING THE BLINDFOLD

Table of Contents

Preface

Enthusiasm and frustration are the parents of this writing and, like all good parents, they have made equal contributions to nurturing its growth. Enthusiasm plays its part as I am fascinated by the application of analytical thinking in a practical way to the world around us in general, and to business endeavours in particular. I also enjoy the creativity and satisfaction of drawing together structured projects. This book, representing some four years of reflection, consultation and development, is one such project – and certainly one of my most fulfilling efforts.

Sadly, I have to mention the other parent in less positive tones, like being forced to acknowledge the presence of the embarrassing relative attending a family wedding. Frustration has driven this writing too. All too often I see undue credibility given to false arguments and unquestioned evidence. A malign influence extends across all areas of life as the many different examples provided so clearly demonstrate.

The quality of analysis which swirls around us via the various media platforms and means of communication is strikingly shallow and poor – far more so than most people, including professionals, actually realise. Recommendations which arise are limited in scope and effectiveness, and we all lose out in terms of wealth, opportunity and quality of life.

I hope, therefore, that this particular child will do what so many children do: keep asking the 'why' question. Only by adopting critical thinking can we become dissatisfied with inadequacy and expediency, and discriminate between the alluring and the effective.

Alan Wood
Birmingham, United Kingdom

Section 1: Why Critical Thinking

As I'm writing this introduction I have the television on in the background – a wallpaper of sound around the room beyond the computer screen. According to the ever-breathless TV news presenters, the main story right now is the economy: the fiscally-sick Eurozone with Greece in dire straits and other member countries in varying degrees of trouble. The United Kingdom, following in America's footsteps of credit overspends and mortgage insecurities, faces either a double dip recession or, best case scenario, a shallow recovery with few new jobs being created for the foreseeable future. Ultimately all this is happening because in previous years there was a massive failure in the business and political sectors to use critical thinking in day to day decision-making. Greed, emotion and hubris reigned.

1.1 Critical Thinking – a definition

Critical thinking (CT) is the process of systematically, fully and accurately understanding an issue, specified problem, or set of information. This approach ultimately permits effective responses to be enacted, based on the highest quality of informed and unbiased decision-making.

This broad and functional definition means that CT can be described justifiably as a set of highly transferable skills. CT can be used across professions, projects and enterprises, and at all levels of decision-making or supervision.

1.2 Critical Thinking – its organisational importance

CT provides nothing less than a cornerstone, the key point which provides support and around which the rest of the structure is built. Or, to change the building metaphor, it is the solid foundation upon which strong, durable walls can be built up. So it is with CT: its presence makes possible so much else.

This is not just over-enthusiastic hyperbole. Neither is it a cynical sales pitch to create a new management-training niche for profitable marketing to the gullible. Rather, just a short time of reflection will confirm the cornerstone or foundation metaphor as a reasonable picture of CT's significance.

After all, any organisation can be healthy if it is practising

14

- Strategic thinking and niche leadership

- Creative thinking and innovation

- Collaboration and team building

- Communication and influence

Now let's relate this checklist to the definition of CT given above. Strategic thinking arises from a clear and detailed view of a situation; that same high level thinking identifies new needs and exploits them quickly, creating niche leadership (and highly successful branding along the way). Full understanding of a situation provides the mundane but necessary starting point for questions behind creative thinking and innovation; emotion and process – aspects of CT which are just as significant as quantitative data – enable effective collaboration and positive team building.

The last bullet point on the checklist requires a little more attention because of a commonly repeated failure by managers and directors. Clarity of information and an appropriate explanation of its significance between them promote effective communication and influence. So often, however, directors and line managers confuse frequency of transmission with real communication: each memo, every e-mail repeatedly fails to provide proper situation reports, briefings notes and/or actions with task rationales and monitoring arrangements. And then senior staff wonder why their subordinates' responses are confusing or incomplete...which of course provokes yet another round of equally inadequate messages to the staff. In short, internal communications becomes inefficient and ineffective, a massive and needless waste of paid time and resources.

The value of CT both for companies and for individuals is clearly demonstrated by its inclusion and importance within psychometric testing, especially for the crucial decision-making responsibilities of management.

1.3 Critical Thinking – answer to commercial pain

From all this, it is unsurprising to believe that improving CT abilities is, 'one of the most obvious and valuable things companies can do to improve their bottom line'.[i] The clear message is that we must use CT as a primary tool to grow our businesses. Such analytical skills address the causes of commercial pain and turn potential into profit.

Commercial pain, broadly speaking, divides into the two categories of reduced profitability and poor staff capabilities. These are keenly felt at the best of times and need to be addressed ruthlessly to take companies forward. During recessions and recoveries, however, they can strike a fatal blow to a business. They are not independent: profitability suffers when staff capabilities are limited and morale is low. Frankly, cutting the training budget at highly pressured, competitive times is not just like shooting yourself in the corporate foot – it is blowing out your business brains.

Key personnel may possess inadequate skill sets - a range of abilities, training and experience which do not correspond with company needs. They may be mismatched either in terms of skills mix or levels of competence. Skills gaps and weaknesses in turn result in confused decision-making, poor and inconsistent problem solving, and failure in collaboration with teams or projects - risking collapse without micromanagement by senior staff. Resourcefulness, creativity and innovation become noticeable mainly by their absence. Competitive edge is lost as product features and services are overtaken by rivals' methodical development and focused marketing. In such circumstances, the company's survival prospects are bleaker than the Mordor landscape in Tolkien's Lord of the Rings.

1.4 Critical Thinking – competitive advantages for businesses

But what if these fundamental needs are tackled systematically within a company through investment in critical thinking skills? Let's look at the basics by laying out a summary of the profitable advantages which arise from deploying staff equipped with CT skills. We can do this by grouping positive behaviours and approaches which arise from particular aspects of CT. We can then match such key positive changes in staff competences with the kinds of strategically profitable advantages that businesses need.

Clarification: CT skills which reveal full and true information despite potentially influential 'masking' or 'overlay' by other factors. This grouping can include distinguishing fact from opinion, recognising attempts to persuade to one particular interpretation ('spin'), and balancing logic and emotion. The resulting behaviours include a healthy scepticism concerning 'pundits' and a confident ability to push back against strongly expressed opinions; recognising and labelling other people's agendas; avoiding hasty conclusions and recommendations; and asking further questions which aid a full factual understanding.

Strategically profitable advantage: More effective problem-solving with clear definition of core issues.

Evaluation: CT skills which promote an accurate assessment of information. This grouping brings together identification of assumptions and inbuilt bias, weighing up data appropriately, scrutinising arguments/data for accuracy and relevance, and correctly handling visual information (using diagrams to represent protocols, concepts and sets of data). Behavioural outcomes from acquiring such skills include the abilities to apply criteria to assessment work, to identify what is known and what isn't, to thoroughly consider all aspects of a proposal, to adjust assumptions in the light of new knowledge, to understand how conclusions and recommendations are formulated, and to develop viable protocols, proposals and sales pitches.

Strategically profitable advantages: Improve decision-making and communication skills; and strengthen strategic planning and creative skills.

Collaboration: CT skills which utilise a 'broad view' mindset. This outlook involves contributing to, and drawing ideas and information from, departments or disciplines or multiple sources. The result is a readiness to seek and explore different perspectives actively, and an ability to handle uncertainties and apparent contradictions.

Strategically profitable advantages: Effective and sustainable team building with actionable outcomes.

Once you think through the skills, behaviours and outcomes given above, it is evident we are talking about nothing less than long-term sustainable, improved profitability. There are, of course, the obviously linked financial benefits we most easily recognise: increased sales, increased customer satisfaction/retention and more effective negotiation with company suppliers.

However, there are also the significant 'backroom' cost savings such as reduced customer acquisition costs, efficient workplace operations and communications, and avoiding the waste of vital investment funds drawn into inappropriate product development and marketing strategies.

And there is the bonus of staff who, being trained to question and move beyond assumptions, are actively seeking opportunities to innovate and adapt – and want to do so. Morale rises as they are affirmed through the additional training investment and potential advancement. Doesn't that sound like a business worth developing?

1.5 Critical Thinking – making it work for you

You also need to understand right from the start that CT is very much an applied skill. You get better at it by making a commitment to use the techniques you learn in the situations you face every day. So this tome is far from being a piece of Nobel-winning literature; instead, it is a handbook with contents designed to plug in and use immediately in your current role and with your current procedures. It does not explore some of the theoretical discussions concerning the formation of arguments but does tell you how to 'spot and stop' where it really counts and costs.

The illustrations have been chosen from inside and beyond the world of business; they have been selected to communicate as clearly and simply as possible the concepts and tactics which the reader can then apply to their individual situation. The challenge of doing so makes the process of reading through this book much more active and self-reflective than would otherwise be the case. They also look out beyond commercial "net curtains" into the wider world in order to pique curiosity, maintain the interest and thus reinforce the concentrated attention which is needed to recognise and break slack thinking habits.

And so we come to the title of the book, "Lifting the Blindfold". By putting into practice what is shared in this volume, you will see around you much more clearly than ever before– you will be better able to understand what is really happening whenever and wherever business is done, and have an unhindered view of decision-making and communications when competitors are still handicapped by their lack of thoroughly applied critical thinking skills. A blindfold which many, in fact, do not even realise they are wearing.

Section 2: Foundations

Common and Situational Assumptions

Deploying CT skills enables you to structure and develop evidence and counter-arguments. Putting this into practical terms for the business sector, this covers assessments, reviews, proactive presentations, viewpoints and projections. Section 1 has described the various strategically profitable advantages for CT at organisational level but they arise from the sum of the individual efforts of the staff. So what does CT look like at individual level? What should you be learning for day-to-day work demands?

2.1 Components

As a recognisable core skill of the commercial world, CT incorporates[ii]:

- Understanding and applying definitions in a disciplined way
- Examining assumptions and distilling facts from opinions and prejudices
- Gathering and organising (structuring) relevant information, calculations and sources

- Analysing - identifying and taking apart ideas, arguments, data and anecdotal evidence and assumptions
- Demonstrating an open attitude towards correlations, facts and responses
- Interpreting relationships between information and the significance of events or thresholds
- Articulating inferences (stating projections, options and implications derived from the evidence sources)
- Being open to self-questioning during the CT process:
- Recognising and challenging invalid arguments
- Retaining the context of, and focus on, the primary issue
- Drawing conclusions based on the information, interpretations and qualifications/ status of expert participants
- Explaining – conveying evidence-based reasoning without ambiguity
- Forming justifiable recommendations and/or action plans

To say the least, this is a list which demands a lot of the would-be critical thinker. That is not the same as saying it is impossible, however, and the following chapters provide plenty of applications of all the above components. This is just like taking the effort to raise the hand and pull hard to loosen the blindfold once you understand it is there, tight over your eyes.

2.2 Self-questioning and clarity

The list above reflects the degree of self-discipline which is always required for effective questioning. This is a real challenge as it is an attitude, not just an approach. Objectivity is an aspiration rather than a fully-realised truth for each one of us. Too often instead we suffer from something like 'white coat syndrome': in discussions we cling on to a stereotypic mental image of ourselves as scientists with clipboards standing around and exuding an air of dispassionate observation. We underestimate our own subjectivity, and can fail to give due credit to the straight thinking of others.

Instead, we have to adopt a willingness and discipline to monitor our own performance in matters of analysis. We must consciously question our personal assumptions, biases and formed opinions and we should have the openness mentioned earlier to reconsider interpretations and judgements. We will need to remain focused on what is required irrespective of personal values or reactions, demonstrating due diligence in structuring cases for or against each one of the full range of available options.

I would hope that this is not me just preaching from my soapbox. CT requires a professional commitment far beyond learning a list of tricks and tactics for making successful arguments or presentations. The detail is provided in the book but the right attitude is always provided by the reader.

Clarity, however, is all about effective communication. We want – and need - others to be able to follow immediately what is being said and why it is being said. We must create a seamless sequence from first stating the intention or proposition, through reviewing credible evidence (information, examples) and demonstrating why it validates conclusions, before finally developing recommendations, priorities and action plans.

2.3 Common assumptions[iii]

The starting point for building up CT skills is a broad understanding of assumptions. Assumptions fall into two types: '**common**' and '**situational**'. We will return to situational assumptions in the next part of the book but for the moment let's consider the 'common' category. First of all, a basic definition: common assumptions are general or collective conditions which apply to CT-based arguments. There are several such assumptions which may not even be obvious – but they exist and make their presence felt through what can be argued or analysed and how it is done.

Listeners/audience: The first of these common assumptions is that all those taking part in a discussion function as a 'participatory audience' whether they realise it or not. They are not passive witnesses to a declaration but actively proposing information and interpreting what is being heard.

Within a business context, defining the people attending an ordinary departmental meeting or scheduled working group as an 'audience' seems less obvious than for one-off public and political speaking, charity events and so on but the real key is the word 'participatory'.

No matter how inert an attendee may appear to be on the outside, on the inside the mind is still engaged. They may or may not be applying CT skills to this engagement – indeed, a lack of concentration may mean that very little of the meeting's content may be subjected to any degree of CT. (And this is doubly true of departmental meetings on Friday afternoons...!). Their contributions will be affected by the quality of their understanding and analysis.

The ability of the participants to listen and argue through the means of CT is a vital factor in outcomes of such meetings. As will become evident, tricks of communication are highly effective when a skilled proponent of a viewpoint is familiar with the personal agendas, expectations, priorities, emotional baggage/intelligence and frank prejudices of their listeners. The informed proponent can therefore select examples and arguments which confirm people in their thinking. Knowing the 'audience' in this way enables them to anticipate the most likely responses and thus 'get their retaliation in first'.

The word 'participatory' has additional significance when there is such a proponent in action. The business 'audience' is not expected to be supine or passively absorbing like sponges and one of the basic requirements of the chair person is to ensure that no-one leaves the room without having been heard . A skilled proponent, by knowing the 'audience', will try to ensure that as much of that input as possible will reinforce his/her particular point of view or proposition. Note that 'skilled' in this context could also be replaced by 'devious'.

Possibilities: The next common assumption is that of 'openness'. This means there is an understood possibility that things *can* be different. It follows that inference can provide such differences and new directions (i.e. statement or fact X suggests Y is true/possible).

Openness can have a second meaning as an assumption: namely, that traditional, extreme, or ineffective solutions are all vulnerable to being discounted. Optimisation is a key outcome for businesses through the openness assumption. We should note that this second meaning also depends in part upon knowing the audience (and its likely response) in order to have some idea of what constitutes 'extreme' for that particular context.

Furthermore, this second meaning has to be somewhat tentative because in one sector, that of business turnarounds and recovery, an 'extreme' position or plan might actually be the most justifiable option, removing people from approaches and business cultures which have failed miserably so far.

Rationale: Following on from uncertainty, there is an assumption of 'rationale' being adopted as a central tenet for critical thinking processes. Openness recognises that there are degrees of uncertainty as we have just mentioned; a careful judgement of factors or information is required in order to progress through this uncertainty to a conclusion and recommendation for action. This judgement process in turn is what is meant by 'rationale' (also termed the justification). It can be summarised in general by the statement:

Rationale = evidence + reasons for making inferences.

Placing rationale centre stage may seem a little surprising at first. Perhaps we would automatically assume that data and other information would occupy such a position. However, a moment's reflection suggests otherwise. Information, interpretations and correlations will change as circumstances and risks also evolve into new and perhaps unanticipated forms. What remains constant, though, is the principle that an explainable, evidence-based judgement has to be developed whatever the information which is available at time of analysis.

Shared goals: Sometimes another type of common assumption is proposed, that of all participants in an argument 'sharing the goal of reaching the truth'. Whatever the setting, I have always felt that there exists a tension – if not an outright contradiction - in applying critical thinking with this assumption as part of the framework for business CT.

After all, why should we assume that all participants in a discussion or dispute or competitive presentation are looking for the same outcome, an identical 'truth' of best choice? Realistically, quite a lot of critical thinking skills are directed specifically against the practice and consequences of deception or bias, and not all of these tactics are accidentally or sub-consciously deployed. Only in science-fiction, it seems to me, does there exist some higher order of (usually alien) being, willing to uphold and share benign communal enlightenment for the advancement of all.

Unless there has been an unusually successful bout of team building, this last assumption can be set aside in favour of more realistic views of the human factor. A **'shared goal of argument'** may exist only as an ideal which is politically correct to espouse for teamwork. The more likely assumptive framework includes **'recognition'** instead – acknowledging the powerful forces of agendas, ambitions, non-rational thought or prejudices, income and status, ego and self-glorification are ever-present in commercial undertakings as with other human endeavours.

In this less than perfect way, the 'shared goal of argument' comes down to strategic aims and objectives in fulfilment of company mission statements. Even so, at lower levels of management, approved activities and tactics may reject rather than establish common agreement as to best options and recommendations.

Other definitions of a 'shared goal' where it can be argued to exist may depend upon the established cultural or wider professional boundaries of ethics and behaviour – any solutions have to operate within these parameters. The critical thinker does not have to fear that their rare skills will be redundant any day soon.

2.4 Situational assumptions[iv]

Having spent some time on common assumptions we now need to greatly improve our understanding of the presence and power of situational assumptions. A limited comprehension only encourages us to respond to challenges in weak ways, believing these are our only options and that, because of those limited choices, we can only have limited influence or success. Without reflecting upon the nature of situational assumptions, we run the risk of perpetual under-performance and under-achievement.

'Situational' assumptions, as the term implies, are found within the detail of particular arguments rather than forming the conditions in which critical thinking can take place.

A situational assumption is 'a supposition that is immediately accepted as truthful.' It may be stated explicitly or implied by information provided as part of an issue in question. It may not even be recognised at all as an assumption at all because, "Everyone knows that ..." The main difficulty is that it is difficult to spot in the first place without disciplined reflection about the arguments or dissecting the links being made between statements.

Take as an example the following theoretical argument: "The continuing demand for rare minerals in the world is increasing as mobile phones and other technologies become more affordable across the globe. Economists are concerned that, especially with China's near-total monopoly on extraction and supply from its territory, other sources are going to run low before new ones are identified. Calls to reduce purchases and replacements in western societies are ignored; the unrestrained promotion of cell phone technology rather than landline services by regional and multinational providers in emerging countries contradicts the need for limiting consumption."

From the last sentence, a major situational assumption is that the promotion (magazine, television and internet adverts, giant billboards and sales kiosks lining the roadsides of African cities) directly feeds all consumer demand. Yet this statement, or something of similar meaning, does not appear as part of the chain of thinking in the last sentence of the example. The assumption is invisible, unrecognised – but still there, regardless.

2.5 The QEP triangle

A simple model demonstrates the central role and key significance of common and situational assumptions – the QEP triangle. For our purposes it is convenient to divide critical thinking issues into three aspects or facets: **Quantity**, **Emotion** and **Process**.

Quantity covers those analytical points which involve figures and measurement techniques. Emotion discusses ways in which feelings influence perceptions and confuse objectivity. Process examines pitfalls in the development of arguments and the consideration of alternatives. All three of these aspects are prone to false and/or unrecognised assumptions undermining the integrity of the thinking.

Each of these aspects –Quantity, Emotion and Process - forms one side of a triangle which represents CT. Sitting in the middle of the triangle are the common and situational assumptions, indicating their influential role in all of the aspects. It is this QEP triangle model which provides the organisation of the main content of the handbook: Quantity – sections 3 to 7, Emotion – sections 8 and 9 and Process – sections 10 and 11.

Section 3: The Truth Is Out There

Context Deficiency

Context here means setting what is known alongside other facts or legitimate comparisons. The lack of relevant facts or comparisons – through insufficient research, neglect, psychological mechanism or deliberate decision - is 'context deficiency'. The term includes incomplete data, omission, over-simplification and the two cultures of 'quantitative vagueness' and 'not looking'. These are all pressure points reflecting complacency, uncritical attitudes or, at its worst, the promotion of individual agendas.

3.1 Incomplete data

Insufficient data does more than prevent meaningful comparisons. It can also limit follow-up and leave unexplored new avenues of enquiry which can clarify the primary issue. Let's consider how we can identify further information needs by logical process and general knowledge, both of which are legitimate management tools.

As a starting point for a demonstration of this process let's imagine that a pension business umbrella group,

"Oldies-Will-B-Us", has produced a worrying market overview on saving up for a comfortable retirement. Its findings are as follows:

- 62% of the over 50's in the UK are paying into a retirement pension.

- 45% of 30 – 50 year olds are paying into a pension.

- 47% of those it has surveyed are failing to make 'adequate provision' for their retirement.

- 44% - 54% of those surveyed each year have failed to make adequate provision during the previous five years.

- An 'adequate pension' is a minimum 10% of earnings each year.

On the surface it would seem that the younger age group are falling behind older people in saving for retirement. A long-term 'poverty in old age' crisis may be developing – obviously a crucial issue of widespread interest to society, both the present generation and the next one (because of national insurance and tax implications).

Some additional information buried within the depths of the report document seems to indicate that the problem is not temporary but is establishing itself quite firmly: the

47% figure for inadequate saving behaviour is consistent with the findings of the previous five years.

Neither is this assertion about consistently failing to save what is needed for retirement merely an administrative word trick. The pension provider applies a standard definition ('minimum 10% of earnings') across all the annual figures for the last few years; this measure helps to confirm the trend.

All this data is quite detailed and helpful as far as it goes, but we could always use more information and ideas in order to fully develop an understanding of the situation. Some of this will come from outside the report itself. For example, from general principles, we might expect that the 30 – 50 age group traditionally saves less for pensions than older people because:

- This is the demographic that is raising children from birth to university or work (if they are lucky enough to have a job these days). This is an expensive and time consuming process often carried out at least for a time with only one partner earning a full income.

- Mortgages and rents are primary concerns of most 30 -50s – with many towards the more expensive end of the accommodation markets because of the aforementioned offspring. I grant you that wealthy DINKies (double income, no kids) are a notable exception here, and have become a growing demographic in the western world, but the general truth still holds for the majority of us. In recent years mortgages have risen from 3x annual income to 5-6x that figure.

- High deposits are often required to move from rental to property ownership. This means a longer period in which disposable income is tied down in targeted savings for deposits rather than being invested in pensions.

- There is also the psychological effect operating as those between 30-40 years do not easily perceive, let alone respond to, the retirement issues and costs which lurk beyond the horizon of getting older. (Before we become too judgemental, many of us can remember when we believed that 40+ was just too old to contemplate...)

We are not quite finished yet with identifying where more information is needed in order to complete an understanding of the primary issue. Arguably, 30 – 50 is a very wide age range in which circumstances and attitudes change much more than in the 50+ age group where there is a greater degree of certainty and life planning.

We have to ask whether a 30 year old really is going to think about the urgency of pensions in the same way as a 49 year old?

What happens if we do the opposite and break down the ages into a series: 30 -39, 40 -49, 50 – 59, and 60 -69? Do we find a slowly increasing trend towards pension provision after all? And how do the figures and percentage changes match those of previous eras? This is another issue which may need to be researched in order to provide the fullest possible context.

Only with all this information gathered together can we truly state with confidence whether a problem really exists, describe its extent and observe where the difficulties lie within such broad age groups and wide-ranging factors. Then, and only then, can an effective policy response be formulated.

3.2 Omission

Omission by neglect is less of an issue for detailed technical reports within business than it is for the gathering of generally relevant information from outside sources. Again, sales pitches are prone to omission if they are drafted in part on information sourced from the public domain. The research itself may be incomplete when it is being drawn from un-coordinated sources and the internet itself, as noted elsewhere, promotes much that is inaccurate and fanciful alongside what is legitimate and confirmed.

Monitoring, evaluation and exit strategy assessments are also vulnerable to straightforward omission but in these instances more depends upon the systematically applied diligence and initiative of the responsible managers involved.

Let's analyse a strategic marketing scenario as an example of simple omission. A confederation of tourism service providers in glorious Sunnyshire points out that tourist numbers in the county have dropped by more than 250,000 during a 3 year period, representing an 10% fall. In response to these figures, local trade bodies call for more government effort and investment in marketing Sunnyshire as a visitor destination. At first sight this looks like progressive leadership and, given the role of tourism as a contributor to the economy as a whole, a real attempt to address a significant problem.

Difficulty, though, arises in correctly defining issues and objectives, and thus where and how much to invest in a new marketing strategy. The message of these figures becomes greatly modified if, upon closer enquiry, it turns out that the three years actually spanned three exceptional summers with low rainfall and high daily sunshine (numbers of hours) figures. The unusually welcoming weather could draw visitors elsewhere as the Sunnyshire tourism industry has a heavily weighted proportion of novel indoors facilities such as climbing walls, artificial pot-holing centres, and dry ski runs. It may also have been relying on receiving a high proportion of week-end/short stay visitors. The latter are very likely wait to see what the more certain short-term weather forecasts are saying before making a final decision to travel.

The background 'baseline' in such a scenario also requires attention. If the three years fall within an economic downturn, tourist figures across the whole country have probably fallen as more holiday makers cut their family budgets. Whilst it is true that just because others are also suffering does not mean that you should as well, it does mean that (a) the impression of isolated crisis is some-what misleading for an investment prioritisation and (b) this information suggests that outdoor or cheaper indoor activities might be a growth component of any eventual response, balancing the portfolio of choices. These concepts are much more commercially focused with viable practical targets than a general outcry for political leaders and their ministries to 'do something'.

So, the actual situation is one which reflects a particular combination of weather conditions and lack of affluence, with a manageable response to both factors.

Anecdotal evidence also provides opportunities for omission. A single experience or reported incident – or even 'a few' (quantitative vagueness applies!) – may not represent the whole body of evidence. Anecdotes, as any monitoring and evaluation officer will say, may indicate how and why something that has been observed is happening, and raise ideas for further questions. They complement measurable data but do not supplant analysis and are vulnerable to the shortcoming termed 'the vividness effect' (section 8).

So far in our discussion of omission we have not considered intentional, calculated and elective use of information or '**cherry picking**'. To be clear, this malpractice is far less gentle and picturesque than the term itself sounds. Neither does the critical thinking term 'fallacy of incomplete evidence' adequately reflect the intellectual – and arguably, moral – dishonesty involved. Consciously directing attention towards carefully selected examples, figures and facts which confirm one particular assertion whilst ignoring known but contradictory data is nothing less than the wilful suppression of evidence. Such a type of omission is dangerous not just because it can create severely misleading and influential impressions; it can do so with only a minimum of effort.

Consider a private consultancy company which, in a press release accompanying the inevitable trade survey, states that 35% of its client market, upon being asked if the business advice they receive is sufficient, indicates they want more. The release, however, fails to mention that a larger proportion – 60% of 2000 participants – have confirmed during the same survey that they don't want any more information; existing provision is sufficient. The second piece of information changes the perception for marketing opportunities, cost-effective investment – and the need for more contracts with the consultancy company.

Cherry picking can be addressed most effectively only if the full range of facts and sources of additional information are to hand but, fortunately, there is a first defence available. If the weight of evidence in support of a review, strategy or presentation has little or no qualification or caution, then this could in itself indicate an instance of the 'fallacy of incomplete evidence'. Certainly, it would be appropriate to ask for sources so that independent checks can be made. An internet search using key words soon reveals whether or not there is more to be investigated.

This leads into the second defence, thorough research, by which all the relevant information can be brought forward in a structured way. Here, we do still have to exercise caution: it is not enough to provide only examples or facts which support an alternative viewpoint. What is being created is a situation in which two opposite but still selective sets of arguments are being proposed. And both may still be missing crucial information which raises other options and recommendations. This situation is a classic illustration of a traditional saying in law circles: "There are two sides to every story – and then there's the truth!"

The correct way forward is to have complete sets of data, presented wherever possible with absolute numbers and ratios which take into account the existence of apparently opposed examples. More detailed statistical analysis is even better if such data is available but at even a basic level of information the point can be made successfully that the original proposition was deceitful. The advantage of having gathered more complete information is that it can move the participants forwards from rejection of the misleading to strategy and planning.

3.3 Confirmation bias

Perhaps the most important factor in overlooking information is that of being human. At its most extreme, we have the example of the pundit style of management and leadership. However, we all filter information with a degree of bias – we have favourite sources of information such as news and business channels, newspapers and journals, blogs and personal contacts. We will turn up the radio when we agree with a presenter's opinion and switch it off or change channels when we disagree. Our very selection of such favourites may restrict or rule out the arrival of certain information before our eyes and minds – and before the next planning meeting.

There is a term which covers this consistent tendency to pick out only the evidence that seems to support our preconceived views, values and assessments: "confirmation bias".

Confirmation bias is extremely powerful, as will be understood from the following list of failings for which it can be responsible:

- Undergirding the persistence of ideas, opinions and recommended actions even when evidence exists against them and has been brought forward

- Accepting lower standards of evidence for currently-held views than is being demanded for assertions which contradict those views

- Re-framing weak and ambiguous evidence as much stronger support for the preconception involved than can ever be justified by dispassionate analysis

- Readily denying the possibility of alternative options, or discarding them when raised, as focus falls on only those possibilities that are consistent with current beliefs

- Increasing resistance to changing strategy because the basis of further analysis finally becomes the professional cost of being seen to be wrong (embarrassment and reduced credibility, practical consequences of accountability)

- Encouraging progressively entrenched attitudes in negotiations as each side involved becomes convinced unjustifiably that it has the strongest position

- Imposing bias so quickly in verbal communications that the hearer is already forming conclusions long before the speaker has shared all the relevant and perhaps contradictory information and reasoned, structured conclusion

46

All this adds up to poor quality options and inappropriate/ineffective decision-making in whatever field of endeavour is involved.

I have spent some time covering confirmation bias because of its strength and its far-reaching effects. With this awareness, however, an individual can critically judge both sides of an argument before coming to a conclusion. In practice, the analytical thinker can utilise a '**devil's advocate' strategy**: imagine that the worst outcome has actually happened (collapse of a project, marketing campaign has failed to raise funds, etc) and then ask why this could be so. The '**5 Whys**' technique mentioned elsewhere is a particularly appropriate and rapid tool for this task.

That last suggestion leads us neatly into the practical application of this omissions discussion to several sectors of managerial responsibility. These include performance management, appraisal processes and continuing professional development. The key to such application is the concept that we all display particular biases or tendencies in which we gain, receive and interpret information and judgements about ourselves. These self-serving mechanisms are really forms of confirmation bias which we apply to our identities and sense of self-worth.

The first such tendency is **self-verification** which is defined as an inbuilt motivation to strengthen the current self-image. The second bias is **self-enhancement**, the inbuilt desire to seek and accept only positive feedback.

As long as a performance assessment or comment is positive, then, there is unlikely to be a problem for a line manager or mentor as they provide feedback and guidance. It is when the comment is negative that communications and operational difficulties of very basic kinds can arise.

People will fail to remember points or ascribe the degree of importance that they should when feedback conflicts with how people see their own personalities, status, talents, values and achievements. Instead, negative feedback – no matter how justified by hard facts - is 'rationalised' as being far less reliable than any positive comments which boost self-esteem or a central role in proceedings. Negative feedback is therefore more readily set aside by the recipient and the practical implications are not put into action.

In addition to the struggle to encourage behaviour change and performance improvement, the status and credibility of the line manager can also come under direct threat as a result of these tendencies. An employee will listen more willingly to a line manager who makes positive comments about the worker's contribution or results. A preference for the actual person who gives favourable feedback becomes progressively reinforced.

This means that a line manager who is equally competent but who needs to address some negative aspect of performance will not communicate effectively. This is not the fault of the supervisor but of the employee: the latter will downplay or rationalise away the correctional messages (even to the extent of valid criticism being perceived as personal attack).

Behaviour will remain unchanged or modify only after a long delay – both of which make the employee inefficient for a period of time. The bias will also break down teams and threaten leadership control in task group settings.

The practical response is for all senior staff and supervisors/line managers to adopt the same 'Sandwich' model of feedback. This communication tool is frequently used in high pressure personal guidance situations such as teacher training and mentoring.

The formula or sequence of discussion concerning performance quality is:

first positive observation + suggested improvement + second positive observation

Assistance for internalising the difficult point(s) can also be provided by asking the non-threatening question:

"How do you think your session went?" This needs to precede the sandwich formula as the line manager or mentor can then incorporate the recipient's own perceptions into the detail of the feedback; it also gives an early opportunity to check the recipient's messages through body language (section 9).

3.4 Primacy effect

As well as confirmation bias itself, there exists another mechanism whereby some information is retained or given undue weight compared to the rest of the available data. This is called the 'primacy effect'. In actual fact, there are two types of primacy effect: **memory** and **irrational**.

The memory version of primacy effect is relatively simple and can be described quickly. Here, the first few points in a series of facts or recommendations are retained more strongly in the memory than later points. In terms of performance, the earlier information is brought back to mind quicker and/or with greater accuracy than the rest of the material.

The irrational primacy effect refers to information being given – quite unconsciously - a disproportionately higher significance in the mind for no other reason than it features early on in a sequence of statements or facts.

Now consider how someone is introduced to another by a third party at a typical business networking event. The primacy effects together would mean that a person who is introduced right at the start of informal mingling and with positive comment immediately forms the strongest impression in the minds of others. Accordingly a business person can maximise their networking effectiveness by making sure they are the first person to be introduced at a meeting to a potential key contact, especially if the friend at their elbow is providing a glowing reference.

The 'know, like, trust' model of business relationship building, in theory at least, may therefore be somewhat influenced by such effects. And in turn, of course, it is often direct personal relationships which can determine the go ahead for joint ventures, referrals and resourcing.

Irrational primacy effect also has tremendous implications for the structure of presentations and report summaries, specifically for the effective communication of key points. '**Frontloading**', with the most vital figures or the most important USPs being mentioned ahead of the rest of the content, would seem to be the best strategy here.

Being aware of the irrational primacy effect, then, if you are on the receiving end of such material or sales pitches it pays to make a concentrated, conscious effort to scrutinise the relative strengths and merits of **all** the listed bullet points and Unique Selling Points.

One technique to offset the primacy effect is to borrow a practice from basic accountancy. Work through the list of key points one way, take a short break and work through the same list in the opposite direction. Then note each time in terms of weighting what you feel about each point alongside it. The actions of reflection and writing provide the time gap and conscious effort which help combat the effect.

3.5 Over-simplification

"Most people reason dramatically, not quantitatively."
Oliver Wendall Holmes, Jnr

Omission of key facts or arguments can also occur through over-simplification. It is very often associated with populism, campaigning and the instant slogan culture of contemporary western cultures. Calculation can be a means of overcoming simplicity as demonstrated by a business-related example arising from the Icelandic ash-cloud which drifted over Europe during Spring 2011.[v] The issue was air safety and the closure of airspace versus commercial interests in maintaining flight schedules and charters.

First a background explanation: the Civil Aviation Authority and the Met Office use computer models supported or supplemented by scientific measurements to identify 'red zones' where belched-out volcanic ash concentrations are dense enough to put aircraft, crews and passengers at high risk. Following the travel chaos of the 2010 Icelandic eruption with the widespread and seemingly everlasting airspace closures across the Eastern Atlantic and Europe, 4 000mcg per cubic metre of air is now used as the safety threshold to map out 'red zones'. An airline CEO, reacting against the 2011 airspace closures, adopted an impressively eye-catching PR approach to express his view. At a press conference he held up for public contemplation a tiny vial of volcanic ash. In this unarguably effective way he was making the point that the threshold concentration for a 'red zone' is remarkably low.

Such a display, of course, is intended to inspire the question, 'Is that all?' followed by the natural corollary of 'What is the fuss about? – Let's keep the planes flying'. But this PR message, admirably facilitated by a simple and striking visual aid, needs careful scrutiny. Let's work this one out instead of just staring at the small vial.

It is not the small quantity of ash granules in one particular cubic metre that is the issue. An aircraft engine can ingest around 3,000 cubic meters per second (according to an on-line comment)[vi] which works out at approximately one million grains every six minutes. Another contributor added that even if there was, for example, a bypass ratio of 80% then an extended flight would not be wise.

Incidentally, the calculation also raises another unexamined implication: that the violent scouring effect – movement of granules against aircraft engine parts – is not captured by the presentation of inert dirt in a vial.

The visual aid with a single, isolated small quantity of ash, doesn't just by-pass the critical calculation. It illustrates a couple of problems for the critical thinker who is trying to analyse such a situation and recover ground in a strategy meeting or similar decision-making forum.

Firstly, the key role of learning by visual means for which we are wired as human beings is a formidable opponent in itself. Words and numbers can come a poor second in the minds of attendees. Furthermore, we are so used to standardised reports and graphics that anything more unusual in terms of visual presentation will immediately and inevitably impress itself strongly on our minds.

Secondly, in the example above, visual means 'easy communication'. A group was recently campaigning against expenditure on a new high speed rail line (the 'HS2') between London and the Midlands. So how do they get their point across? By putting an inflatable white elephant with HS2 printed on its flank in front of the camer-cameras....an instant, memorable message of massive waste. Other groups lobby about excessive bonuses for city investors and CEOs by wearing pig masks and suits, or posing in front of feeding troughs. It is no coincidence that 'visual sloganeering' is now standard practice for getting your point across.

Sound bites achieve a similar aural effect as an easy summary statement of a position. And here is the dilemma: If you are not careful, providing rebuttal in the form of calculations may appear tedious, pedantic and possibly, just possibly, downright geeky.

Be especially aware that a room full of executives used to handling high level information are still fallible men and women who behave by and large in accordance with the findings of social psychology just like the rest of us. The response therefore has to be carefully structured: as much attention has to be paid to the manner in which the reply is given as to its content. A populist PR approach requires a PR-calculated rejoinder even in the boardroom.

Using a calm and deliberately 'warm' tone with open body language to match, point out that:

(1) The visual aid/other approach being used is striking but that doesn't make it automatically the right answer and immune to proper scrutiny

(2) The situation requires deep and accurate consideration because contracts/cash flow/jobs/expansion plans/key client relationships (delete as necessary!) are at stake

(3) Significant decisions demand substantial arguments

Note a sound bite structure on that last point - something which turns populist PR culture against the original presentation. Then:

(4) Present the calculation and its rationale

(5) Provide the conclusion and recommendation

(6) Repeat point 3 and...

(7) Invite the proponent of the visual aid/other PR approach to comment on the calculations

The above might seem quite prescriptive but the need for such a detailed sequence merely reflects the difficulties of overcoming the strong impressions created by an effectively communicated but simplistic assertion. If the proponent of that view is a naturally charismatic pundit (section 7) then the challenge only increases because of their 'celebrity status' and confidence in delivery. Feel

56

free to copy the sequence on to your smartphone notepad for emergency reference.

3.6 Quantitative vagueness

'Quantitative vagueness' is a very useful descriptive term. It means exactly what it says – blurred, imprecise reference to amounts. In the business world there are three commonly occurring aspects which cause confusion, inefficiency and poor teamwork. They are the sloppy habit of generalisation, the related issue of individual interpretation of degree and, a particular favourite of HR managers, rating scales.

Generalisation: This is the question of exactly – or more precisely, inexactly – how many of something are being discussed. All businessmen should be wary of sweeping statements, analysis and conclusions in documents and presentations put before them. Let's look, for example, at a simple statement which has been repeated times without number since 2008:

"Bankers are greedy". Does this really refer to:

- Most bankers

- Many bankers

- Some bankers

- Several bankers

- A few bankers

Such lazy, shallow thinking can be identified and challenged by inserting the word 'all' into any such assertion and seeing how ridiculous and intolerant it becomes.

There is a more subtle form of this transgression. Be aware that some contributors will use phrases like, "The vast majority....." without analytical support but as a forceful expression of a personal view only.

However strident or subtle, the most practical action is to zero in on any such words and insist on having actual figures – along with research or reasons which support the statistics that are eventually provided.

If you really want to make a point with a particularly slack report or sales pitch then use the word 'all' as suggested but shared with the group at large. You may need to consider the diplomatic consequences, however, before this more drastic step and it might be best if you just mutter 'all?' under your breath...

Degree: this notion follows through the concept of a 'culture of quantitative vagueness' a little further. Even pinning down a 'qualified generalisation' as described above may not significantly improve interpretation and decision-making in practice for settings such as working groups and project teams. This is because relative descriptions are just that – relative. So what do the same terms mean to different people – even those on the same team?

Here is a simple but revealing exercise which can help in answering that last question:

Each team member draws two lines of equal length 10cm across a sheet of paper. The lines are marked 0 at left hand side origin of the line, 5 half-way along the line and 10 at the right hand end.

These figures are just to help make the judgement calls which now follow. Individually – without showing this DIY worksheet to anyone else – every participant writes the words 'most', 'many', 'some' and 'few' where they think they belong on the first line. In the same way, everyone marks their second line for the word 'several'.

The group's results for 'Most', 'Many', 'Some' and 'Few' can be compiled on the first line of another worksheet or all the sheets trimmed and placed under one another on a flat surface. The process can be repeated for 'Several'. The group members can see instantly just how much variation they share between themselves concerning their personal interpretations of the words.

The spread can be quite startling – and alarming when it is remembered that everyone will be unconsciously assuming such words are understood by everyone else in the same way. This really does serve to underline the need for quantitative precision – for actual numbers and justifications for those figures.

Rating scales: In an ironic reversal of the usual kind of problem faced with analytical thinking, there are some occasions when the truth out there is somewhat hidden by too many figures rather than too few.

Sliding or rating scales, beloved by so many managers as a convenient feedback tool, are a common example. 1 – 5 or 1 – 10 rating scales are often used to assess risks or customer/staff satisfaction. However, they reflect reality very imprecisely: they are not ranges based on formal systems of measurement but on very different perceptions. These are highly individual because they are determined by unspoken assumptions, confidence or fear, technical ignorance, particular skill sets and other, immeasurable, factors.

Staff and customer satisfaction surveys based on scales are very limited – perhaps less informative than may be generally understood – because they are not really objective for all these reasons. The significance of grouping sliding scales results becomes even more confused for year on year analysis when you take into account staff turnover, each staff change between times bringing further personal factors into play. Yet sliding scales are treated by managerial minds as scientifically impartial; averages are still calculated and compared to those of previous years with the notion of making decisions based on changes in the (at best) semi-quantitative values.

Sliding scales and their variations certainly can provide pointers for further enquiry but they should not be used in isolation from other information and a good personal knowledge of the staff involved. Project management handbooks can provide mixtures of monitoring and evaluation techniques which together build a true picture and identify priorities.

3.7 Not looking

Those drawn from traditional Catholic and Anglican backgrounds who are familiar with the liturgical prayers of confession will immediately recognise the concept of 'not looking' as an example of doing something wrong by not doing anything at all.

In critical thinking, 'not looking' refers to wrongly upholding an assertion or conclusion simply because no steps have actually been taken to check if the assertion is true or not.

I have a high degree of wariness about reported illnesses and other global statistics. As an example, quite a few countries declared to the World Health Organisation very low levels of leprosy in their populations during the

1980s and 1990s. However, when paramedics, community leaders and others were trained to go into villages and towns to identify the clinical symptoms, the reported rates invariably rose, sometimes to triple or more the official rates. Leprosy was a seemingly low level public health problem, and often poorly funded as a result, because it was not being sought out due to a lack of will or initiative.

The tragedy is that this concerned what is actually an easily treatable, fully curable infection. The information deficit also had a detrimental effect on local commercial suppliers from pharmaceuticals to training businesses which were deprived of a much-needed market.

In business, when someone tells you that 'there is no evidence', the correct response in critical thinking is then to ask, "What measures have been taken to confirm there really are no signs that your assertion is true or qualified?" If that question is followed by an epic silence and a paralysis of taser-induced proportions then you can guess the answer is 'none' and there is further work to be done.

For critical thinking in the business sector, omission, over-simplification and quantitative vagueness may prove to be only the start of presentational issues to overcome within the setting of planning and evaluation meetings. Once the initial facts have been established through the responses discussed in this section, be prepared for a secondary tactic by proponents of the challenged information and conclusions. That tactic is '**shifting ground**' which is more fully explained in section 10.

For the moment it is sufficient to note that once the initial position has been discredited, then a more moderate but still debatable position is taken up and held. The responses discussed later then have to be deployed in order to further move information back on to solid ground. Nevertheless, and particularly in addressing omission, oversimplification and 'not looking' propositions, much of the hard work will have already been done.

Section 4: Common Yet Complicated

Percentages

Percentages are the most common statistics that business people encounter - from broadcast and print media, training courses, reports, assessments, monitoring and evaluation procedures, expert submissions and the rest of daily business life. As with more complex forms of information and means of feedback, you need to be confident that the facts and conclusions are solid enough to act as foundations for growth strategies, market plans, sales presentations and product/service deliveries. Or you need to identify weak, potentially incomplete information in order to defend your company's bottom line by avoiding costly errors. In short, you need to question paperwork and people alike even for this most basic type of data.

Because percentages are such a universal experience we'll treat them as a topic in their own right for simplicity and ready reference. First of all, we need to look at three related issues which concern the presentation of percentages themselves. Here, it is possible to have figures quoted in such a way as to create a misleading impression without anything further being stated. These points must feature in your check list; if you are not convinced by what is in front of you then at least that dissatisfaction will enable you to formulate a question immediately in order to clarify the information being provided.

4.1 Percentage only

Be wary and act dissatisfied whenever someone quotes you a percentage in isolation. The percentage figure should always be accompanied by the corresponding absolute number. A typical way of doing this follows the format: 40% (200), 30% (150) and so on. Only by having the two types of statistic together can you expect to realistically estimate the strength of the evidence and/or the validity of the interpretation.

The same principle applies when percentage changes are quoted. Imagine a company is reported as suffering a 100% increase (a doubling) in bad debt clients this year. That sounds drastic – a catastrophe in the making which needs highest priority focus and perhaps some additional resourcing or staff deployment. However, that figure could be completely insignificant if the company has one thousand clients and the percentage of bad debt clients has gone from 1% to 2% (ie 10 to 20). The firm is hardly in peril as long as those particular 20 people aren't the handful of clients who provide 90% of the business....This is not to encourage complacency towards customers, of course, but much of management is about deploying finite money, time and effort in a structured, prioritised way.

The precautions that you need to take are at least relatively simple and will reward the very modest effort required. So be prepared to challenge all instances of 'percentage only data' in documents, presentations or other briefings that you receive. Request all the original figures from which the percentages are derived and don't forget to set a deadline for receiving them. (The second point is best management practice anyway but also carries a significant message about the seriousness of the omission.) You can then review the collective picture created by all the assembled information or press harder on dubious points arising from the original data.

It is always worth asking any provider of percentages without the corresponding absolute numbers why the latter were not forwarded as they should have been. Posing this question conveys an appropriate message concerning the standards to which you work and expect of others. It may open up further lines of enquiry concerning the quality of information and/or wider circumstances you are addressing – and simultaneously provide a useful impression of the provider's business honesty and competence.

There is a very positive side to this advice too. To improve your own standards of presentation and sales pitches/tenders you absolutely need to ensure that numbers always accompany percentages wherever such statistics are cited. It is amazing how many questions from a potential customer can be anticipated by your sales staff being familiar with all the figures and their background.

4.2 Percentage breakdown (sets) – visuals

Moving on from the occurrence of figures in text, a second occasion when the critical thinker should be wary is when percentages without absolute numbers are presented to them as pie charts or graphs. The strong visual impact of either of these can surprisingly effectively distract you from the fact that you only have half the necessary information to make the best possible decision, and make low and potentially unconvincing numbers much more credible. This can especially be a problem within sales pitches, expenditure summaries and 'quick grasp' reports.

The largest segment of a typical pie chart showing various percentages, for example, gives a strong initial impression that it is not just dominant but highly significant – it implies something substantial lies behind it. You need to be aware that this is a powerful and immediate subconscious message to those who view any pie chart.

But how reliable an impression does the breakdown create if it is then revealed that an impressive 55%, for example, is revealed as just 11 out of a total of 20 units. At this point a wider context is required: is 11 a greater number than might reasonably be expected for that time period? How do you know or measure such a frequency of occurrence? What is the baseline from which change is measured? Big questions must follow small absolute numbers wherever percentages are involved.

This point about visual impact of percentages is really significant. To emphasise the potential strength of a misleading impact created by percentages, have a go yourself at converting the numbers below into two pie charts.

Pie-chart one: 10% (2), 15% (3), 20% (4) and 55% (11)

Pie-chart two: 10% (100), 15% (150), 20% (200) and 55% (550)

You will find that the two sets of very different values give rise to exactly the same pie chart. Yet if we think of these figures as equally valuable income sources or numbers of clients on databases then surely firms would much prefer the second set!

A firm attitude needs to be cultivated both in the minds of subordinate team leaders and other staff towards current and potential suppliers. You should challenge all 'percentage only' data in visual presentations received from other sources. The availability of such full sets of data as those above is not the only issue, of course. Suppliers can prove their competence or otherwise by speedily correcting what should have been shared in the first place. Hesitations, incomplete figures and 'lost information' are perhaps indicators that all is not well in the relationship between the businesses involved.

What does all this mean for good practice and presentation quality? The first point is one of due diligence. You must ensure that all visual presentations for which you are responsible (and those reporting to you according to line management) include both percentages and their absolute figures on the chart/graph itself. For best practice, these should be positioned as close as possible to the relevant part of the visual presentation.

An alternative means of achieving the same clarity is to make the percentages and original numbers available in an accompanying list. Again, this list should be placed alongside the chart/graph.

In either case above, you need to make further enquiries to obtain such data wherever the figures are not provided initially. Any review, let alone decision, should be postponed until those enquiries have been successful and it becomes possible to consider the collective picture created by all the assembled information together. This may seem a basic statement but in the heat of deadlines, intense competition and senior management 'time is money' pressures, it is tempting to take risky shortcuts with information gathering. It is therefore better by far to be clear in the mind well ahead of such stressful moments what will be the correct action to take.

So far during discussion about percentages and visuals we have considered the 'must do' and 'must watch for'. It is also important to think about a key 'do not'. DO NOT try to present a whole series of figures and percentages in a turgid paragraph of text. A simple list or table relays figures far more readily with a minimum of additional explanation and a maximum impression of brisk efficiency.

This particular advice may seem basic but is certainly an appropriate reminder to managers who are supervising staff in the throes of preparing presentations for the first few times. And, of course, when an article or book presents useful information in this less-than-helpful way then write out your own table to more thoroughly grasp the figures and conclusions.

4.3 Percentage versus absolute number

This approach, it seems to me, is a particular favourite of politicians making fixed ideological points. However, it may also turn up in review documents as distortions imposed by the selective prism of commentators. It also occurs in general news articles according to the editorial stance of the publishers.

Less likely but not impossible, examples of what I am about to describe may turn up in think tank reports and press releases. It is always useful knowing who are the financial backers and biggest customers of think tanks - a wonderful example of context deficiency.

Having largely avoided it so far, we do need to apply a little bit of maths to understand the full importance of what is being said, and how it is being used to support partisan points. Indeed, it is possible to obscure or tone down the full impact of inconvenient figures in a very "calculated" way; the principle is to report the figures deliberately in this manner so that the reader has to make an additional effort to uncover the truth.

The issue usually arises in a format similar to this: an initial 'whole group number' is stated, and it is then followed by details of percentages:

"Of the organisation X's 300 000 membership, 65% voted for action Y on a turnout of 35%".

It takes a little time to understand that from the information given then 105 000 people actually voted. It turns out that of these 105 000, 68 250 were in favour of action Y and 36 750 were opposed if we apply the percentages supplied. At this point the partisan interpretations come into play: it is likely that those in favour of action Y will emphasise the percentage figure 65%; those opposed will highlight the small absolute number who voted for that action in comparison with the membership total as a whole.

This is a perennial argument in the sector of industrial relations when it comes to strike ballots and consultations Say that the Union of Gadget Tweakers (UGT) has 400 000 members. A newspaper might make a point by reporting, for instance, that, "strike action is backed by 85% of members who submitted ballot papers but **only 35%** of the union's membership **actually voted**."

So there is a subtext from the editorialising elements (highlighted) that only a militant minority (a percentage of a percentage) have supported strike action. The deeper sub text will be that this ballot is therefore less than democratic – a minority creating havoc for the majority. Indeed, to make sure that the essential point cannot be overlooked by even the most casual of breakfast time readers absorbed in crunching their toast or corn flakes, the headline for the piece may bluntly declare something like: "UGT could close down industry – with only 35% turnout".

Another newspaper might adopt different wording and mobilise the inverted commas for the same strike ballot: "The Union of Gadget Tweakers, which represents 400 000 industry workers, has voted 'overwhelmingly' in favour of strike action. Of the 136 500 (35%) who cast ballots, 85% (116 025) voted for industrial action and 15% (20 475) against.

These phrases hide nothing that is relevant to the debate but allows readers to see and check the figures – and form their personal conclusions. Having said that, it is also possible to express a reservation or disagreement (and therefore include an element of editorialising) by putting the word **overwhelmingly** between inverted commas, as in the above example. The use of such commas in this particular way by popular journalism is very common.

Let's take another newspaper's approach to the same event: "Up to 400 000 workers are expected to strike after members of the UGT voted by nearly 6 to 1 in favour of industrial action (35% turnout)".

Interestingly, here the turnout figure turns up last of all. The lead figure of 400 000 + phrasing of 'expected to strike' + ratio coming first could together create a strong subconscious impression of overwhelming solidarity. Only then, right at the end, does a key statistic for understanding just how few are clearly in favour of such action present itself. When this emphasis on the front-loaded figures is accompanied by the UGT General Secretary declaring: "The clear majority in favour of the strike shows that our workers will fight..." then you know that you have a PR war on your hands.

The discussion above has other direct applications in the business world. The first is found in monitoring and evaluation. What happens if progress as measured by SMART objectives and key indicators is not as good as it should be? How can criticism be minimised? Answer – use the whole group number + percentages format outlined above; the worst news can be further 'buried' as the middle or next to last percentage so that it doesn't stand out. The experienced Monitoring and Evaluation officer concentrates equally on all the figures and makes the calculations to counter such a presentational trick.

Beyond the comments on actual performance versus targets in the subsequent report, the issue of how the results are presented can be covered by recommending a clear percentages + numbers format for the future. Conversely, a full set of figures and percentages offered upfront – or at least conveniently placed ready to hand – reinforces a favourable impression of openness and professional competence. It means that members of the same sales team are clear and not confused by the mixed formula given above. It is also basic good business ethics.

Further manipulation of percentage versus absolute number: there is a common malpractice of citing the relative figure (percentage) when promoting the positive aspects of a favoured action, while quoting absolute figures for the negative points.

It could be claimed, for example, that a new cost-saving measure could cut a particular budget line expenditure by 30% but could lead to 5/1000 customers being poorly served. The advantage to be gained seems significantly higher than the small potential loss.

But we need to know the absolute figures for the budget line and associated elements. Then we can calculate the real value of the saving and whether or not the savings are actually less than the potential loss of income. And this would also need to have a wide margin of safety as it is reckoned that every dissatisfied customer tells around 20 other people about their negative experiences.

Bear in mind too that if you come across this particular presentation tactic then it may represent a particular, biased mind set. The first example of the formula may not be the only one and there is no choice but to investigate and complete all sets of figures. The information will always be useful even if consistent bias may suggest that a new supplier or re-training staff are necessary further steps.

The immediate discussion has covered how important it is to complete the mathematics so that all the corresponding figures for percentages are immediately available and in an easily communicated format. However, as was mentioned in passing right at the beginning of this section, it is equally valuable to identify the emphasis and the potential interest/agenda being promoted by each stakeholder in the meeting. What you may find from such reflections or enquiries will provide starting points for further questions and counter-arguments. These test the robustness of a business case, proposal or results quite ruthlessly – but it is your company and livelihood that are at risk if the decisions are being based on superficial considerations.

It is not enough to understand that tactics and deceits can revolve around the calculations and presence/absence of percentages and figures. There is a second major theme to the abuse of percentages: interpretation. In this next part of the section we look at three important points centred around the significance of the reported percentages. Common to these points, a kind of framework is created which deliberately leads the observer towards the conclusion favoured by the presenter even when other views are possible. Indeed, such opinions or options may prove more valid according to the totality of the evidence than those originally offered. This approach is not exclusive to percentages.

4.4 Editorialising

The first sin of interpretation is 'editorialising'. The key here is to consider the wording which accompanies the percentages. Watch for 'only', 'just', 'hardly more/less than', 'barely', 'similar to' or equivalents which can be casually slipped into the text and which may be quite subtle in their psychological effect. There can be more blatant editorial phrases such as 'significantly worse/better than' and 'obviously this means...' which are more easily identified. In all cases, it is necessary to be especially self-disciplined when those siren-like little words are creating an impression consistent with any of your own assumptions, preferences or arguments.

Sometimes a text can reveal editorial bias by the inconsistency of statements in the very same document or article. Consider two statements, laid side by side, which compare companies B and C.

'B significantly outperforms C by more than 1%'

'B is virtually the same as C with the latter only achieving a 3% higher performance'

It is reasonable to conclude that the author favours XXX over ZZZ – and yes, almost unbelievably, I have even come across an article in a graduate-only profession's publication which did just this (twice!). It was not therefore a matter of intelligence but one of straightforward, blinkered prejudice (section 8.4).

What actions can be taken against such bias? One worthwhile exercise is to review or copy the document and systematically delete the editorialising words around the percentages themselves and in the interpretations which occur prior to the final recommendations or summaries. It then becomes possible to focus on the percentage values cited in isolation and look at what they indicate by themselves. In doing this, it is important to remember the earlier point about seeking the absolute numbers which should accompany those percentages.

A similar response is to extract all the comparative statements from the different parts of the text. They can be laid alongside one another as illustrated above to reveal any degree of inconsistency and bias in the interpretation which will require further investigation.

With either kind of analytical exercise any discrepancy between original recommendations and the 'new' stories being told by 'de-editorialised' material is a warning not to proceed with the project until the new directions and options now revealed are assessed.

4.5 Like-with-like (Match Grid)

The simplicity of percentages can provide a rather specialised example of another potential pitfall with direct applications, the 'like with like' comparison. This has powerful implications for the marketing sector, especially niche marketing and policy planning. The business head has to rule the heart over suspected new opportunities and consciously ask, "Does the reported analysis/profile in front of me with its percentages and figures really match the characteristics of what I am scrutinising, promoting, targeting or defending?" The answer to that key question is to find a means of comparing your own information profile(s) against those being cited in the circulating reports or potential market/growth presentations. Such a comparison can be effectively – and rapidly – achieved by setting up a 'match grid'.

Match Grid: first, you prepare four columns with the headings from left to right as: Characteristic, Your analysis (% + number), Other's analysis (% + number), Match Yes/No

Second, under the first column (Characteristic), you then write a series of rows which are denoted as: 1 + *named characteristic*, 2 + *named characteristic*, 3 + *named characteristic* and so on – as many characteristics as can be identified. Each characteristic or factor that you have identified as important for your target market or other purpose is listed in the first column.

Any information that you have about that characteristic/factor is listed in the second column. The percentages and figures from the other source for the same characteristic/factor are placed in the boxes in the third column.

You may have to go back to the raw data from the other source to assign data, ensuring that the figures and percentages reflect as closely as possible the defined characteristic. Any time spent on this third stage is definitely worth it as you gain a really detailed understanding of the information with which you have been provided. This can give rise to all sorts of relevant and practical questions outside of those relating to the match grid itself.

The last column of the grid will help you make the judgement call on the information. It is where you decide whether or not the correspondence is close enough for your purposes. Writing a clear Yes or No for each factor forces you to make a clear-headed assessment of each point and provides a summary balance of pros and cons. It does not totally eliminate the kind of subjectivity discussed elsewhere but it helps reduce the risk of moving away from the evidence available.

At the 'tactical' level the match grid clarifies decision-making by removing percentages and numbers from editorialising text. It is also an effective time management technique with widespread application in strategic development. The grid removes hidden assumptions and documents exactly what is known as opposed to what is assumed, inferred or projected.

4.6 Percentages and context deficiency

Last, but definitely not least, we have a further general challenge to face when dealing with percentages. As well as considering what is put forward within the documents, media reports, presentations and anecdotal evidence which are immediately to hand it is also important to ask, "What else is happening in the background that is linked to percentages and numbers?" This brings us to the concept of 'context deficiency'.

Consider two companies (assuming each is the only one in its respective town), both serving individual customers and both experiencing approximately **1400%** growth over a decade.

Alpha: 2001 number of customers (local population) = 30 (8 500)

    2011 number of customers (local population) = 420 (13 000)

Zeta: 2001 number of customers (local population) = 150 (10 000)

    2011 number of customers (local population) = 2 000 (800 000)

As an exercise, it is worth writing out the information as a table first. Then compare the various figures provided.

Alpha seems far less impressive than Zeta based on absolute numbers that accompany the percentage figure of 1400%. But Zeta is located in an area that went from 10 000 to 800 000 population - explosive urban growth - in same period. In the light of this additional information, how effective in reality are the two firms in recruiting customers from their respective communities?

As with all other scenarios whenever percentages and absolute numbers are cited as changes and trends, it is vital always to ask the question, "What else may be happening?" If you are presenting a sales pitch or Monitoring and Evaluation feedback then having a detailed answer ready ahead of the face-to-face meeting will communicate much more than just the additional facts. The thoroughness will not go unnoticed.

If you are on the other side of the desk and receiving reports about percentages and trends according to the common model above then there is a different exercise to carry out. It is similar to some of those suggested earlier: extract the percentages + numbers at the beginning and end of the trends from the original text. Again, place them in a table which can be drawn up quickly on the computer (or even on the back of an envelope but then you have to scan it into your files!). This assists the analytical thinking with functional clarity and large changes will provoke the "What else?"/"What aren't you telling me?" questions immediately in the absence of additional explanations and footnotes.

On the wider front, consistent background reading of news and market journals – together with the application of what follows in the remaining chapters of this book – is a strong defence against the context deficiency which may be associated with percentages and trends being brought to your attention.

Section 5: The Big Picture

Overviews

There are a number of traps even when we attempt to look at a situation overall. The most common 'big pictures' which businesses utilise are averages, trends, sampling and surveys, and information visualisation. Each of these seems benignly straightforward and helpful at first sight. However, superficial consideration is unwise when these particular information types are also prime tools for trapping the unwary when developing market strategies and identifying further opportunities. The potential for wasted costs and energy is massive if the basic pitfalls of these four forms of data are poorly understood.

These 4 'big picture' sources are the start of overview development. Framing, batching, ratio bias and types of compromise conclusions are further complications which have to be identified and corrected.

5.1 Averages

After percentages, the notion of 'average' must be the most commonly abused and misused element of critical thinking for business. Here is a fact to contemplate: on average, a member of the human race possesses one ovary, one fallopian tube and one testicle. Already you might be suspecting that information preceded by the phrase 'On average' may be less helpful than might first appear......

We do need to be ready to change our language in order to clarify our thinking and improve our analysis. There are three words which have to be understood and which represent three separate concepts:

1. **Mean** = TOTAL value of items/NUMBER of items (This is what is usually meant by **average**)

2. **Median** = MIDDLE value in a smallest to largest sequence of numbers

3. **Mode** = MOST common value

Let's look at the monthly incomes of a self-employed person over 14 months (in thousands of pounds) as an example of the above terms:

2 5 2 3 4 6 8 3 7 3 9 3 6 1

Firstly, let's rearrange the data in ascending order:

1 2 2 3 3 3 3 4 5 6 6 7 8 9

Mean (average) = TOTAL/NUMBER =

$$\frac{1+2+2+3+3+3+3+4+5+6+6+7+8+9}{14}$$

= 62/14 = 4.43 = **£4 430 average income per month**

Median is the MIDDLE value when the data is arranged in order of size. Where there are two middle numbers as here, then median is halfway between those two numbers. Thus:

1 2 2 3 3 3   4 5 6 6 7 8 9

Seven numbers   Seven numbers

So the Median = **3.5**

= **£3 500 /month**

Finally, **Mode** = MOST common value. In the above sequence of monthly earnings, that figure is **3** (occurs four times in the sequence) = **£3 000 /month**

There is a fourth term which is useful for gaining the broadest possible view of what may be happening. That is **RANGE,** which is the difference between the highest and the lowest values. Here: $9 - 1 = 8$ = **£8 000**

Generally, if the figures are presented in graph form, the mean is not in the middle of the range with almost everything else grouped closely around it and just a few values at the extreme high and low ends. Rather, the majority of values (wages, housing prices etc) are significantly less than the mean and only some values exceed the mean figure. The distribution is therefore a bump to the left in the graph and a tailing off line towards the right – a whale shape, if you like, with the head to the left.

Thus, in the UK national average salary is around £26 600 per year. Yet 50% of full time salaries in the UK are below £20 000 per year and around two thirds are less than £26 000. So the mean actually marks a dividing line between the wealthier 1/3 and the poorer 2/3. It is not the divider between two equal segments of the full time salaried population.

In this case the average, so beloved of politicians, trade union leaders, employers' organisations and journalists, is not where most people actually find themselves but is a far higher value and overstates the situation. In the above example, the mean or average exaggerates people's earnings.

I also have to sound a warning at this point about the notion of '**clumping**'. Whenever someone uses the phrase, "On average..." there is an automatic assumption that many – if not most - of the values are grouped tightly or clumped either side of the cited value. This is a totally subconscious impression, and the only sure response is to look hard at the data which provides that mean/average.

This may seem obvious but be aware that the 'clumping' assumption is quite a powerful psychological entity to challenge, and requires effort. It also requires clear communication in any meeting where others may be blissfully unaware of this significant assumption and its influence on their thinking. Only by bringing all the data into the open can this be countered with confidence.

If the mean can prove so misleading, what may help? The median value for the skewed graph is something of a downwards correction towards where the graph 'bulges'. It is not perfect but it is a very useful improvement and 'back of the envelope' type figure for business purposes.

5.2 Trends

Analysis of trends is important not just for understanding how a current situation has developed but also to anticipate near-future events and opportunities. Within this area, certain aspects are particularly important to critical thinking in the business environment, including **sampling period**, the '**recency effect**' and **isolating trends**.

Sampling period is an area of practical concern across business sectors: expert evidences and performance reviews; commercial and economic trends; seasonal patterns and demand cycles; client retention and new client acquisition databases. All require a strict and precise analysis which is not necessarily achieved because of the defined sampling period.

Let's look first at why the sampling period can prove crucial to the interpretation of a situation. A specialist car parts firm income is calculated as only 76 % of the long-term average for the period October to May. This is widely reported within the industry as the worst set of figures for at least five years. Obviously, this is heralding economic devastation and a storm of P45s at the company. Or is this just needless scaremongering?

Whenever someone declares, "These are the worst figures since.....", we need to pose a key question. That question is: "Why sample the specific period quoted?" We need to look at the start and end points, clarify the rationale for the period being used for information or comparison. Crucially we should explore what may have been excluded and how much that changes conclusions or recommendations.

Back to our car parts firm then ... June rather than May is actually the most reasonable end point for a seasonal comparison because it is the last month when seasonal demand remains high for the specialist parts. If June is added on to the end of the specified period we create a realistic and meaningful period for analysis rather than an arbitrary one.

And surprise, surprise! When June is included, the picture changes and the headlines look decidedly overblown. Demand turns out to be 92% of the long-term average for that period. A shortfall of 8% rather than the much-hyped

24% is much less dramatic – and far less newsworthy. Or is that being too cynical?

And what is the vital information about June being a significant part of the pre-summer sales? We haven't been told that the specialist parts are pieces for the removable roof on convertible cars. Demand along the just-in-time supply chain increases in early summer as the peak sales period (with pre-orders) looms. And the dealers know that the family market increases during the July-August summer holidays whilst couples without children buy slightly earlier (June – July) to maximise the use of the new car.

Interestingly, then, the misleading trend period depended for its full effect upon context deficiency, an absence of key relevant facts. This brings out the strong caution that context deficiency may accompany selective trend periods in arguments and assertions.

How do you counter context deficiency when 'you don't know what you don't know' so cannot formulate a direct question? Ask time-based questions instead: "What happened immediately before/after the period you mention?" or "If we added [x period before/after the time mentioned] how would the results differ – and why

As well as challenging the trend period, a second scrutiny is recommended: checking to see if there is a '**recency**' effect. Imagine being told by a sales team during a presentation to you that, "Our business has grown X% over last five years". The intention is to imply they are successful, know what they are doing, have appropriate products/quality - and should be the vehicle of your company's success too. However, the five year period they quote could actually disguise excellent growth for three years followed by gradual decline in the most recent two. Although the end point may still be higher than the beginning you would want to know why the customer base is now shrinking – and ask if it is something that might adversely affect your own business?

The same caution needs to be exercised towards those who claim they or their products are the 'fastest growing X in the last three years'. This could mean they have been world beaters consistently for each of the last three years – or they got exceptionally lucky in only one year. And if that one year is the first of the three......

To counter the 'recency effect', nothing replaces thorough research and posing another awkward question: "Can you give me a breakdown of performance during the period you have just quoted?" You also have to consider how reliable is a trading source, supplier or outlet going to prove when they have already been significantly economical with the economic truth? In business and politics, history is consistently and ruthlessly salami-sliced into short periods which precisely support a marketing promotion, a particular ideology or cause of the week.

The third aspect is '**isolating trends**', whereby there are two (or more) related sets of figures which together give an overall result. However, only one or more of them may be provided for consideration and the other(s) are ignored.

As a quick example, let's return to our specialist car parts firm. It supplies items for convertible models of the Chugg brand. The demand has increased by 1% (year on year rise) through official Chugg dealers. For a continuing weak economy and generally declining car sales, this is a good performance.

However, independent repair shops, dealers and collector clubs are showing a 9% year on year rise as recession-hit consumers look for cheaper outlets. With absolute figures, the full costs and profits can be evaluated but the newly growing market certainly needs investigation if the car parts firm is to adapt to harsher trading conditions.

Again, let's say that a declining economy correlates with an increase in crime – seems reasonable and easy for a proponent to declare as the basis of an immediate poverty-driven crime wave. However, this is not an even trend. Increasing metal thefts mean that recorded burglaries from factories and warehouses have risen by 3% year on year. Yet the same targeting means that burglaries from shops, offices and homes are down by 5% and with absolute figures which more than compensate for the rise in burglaries from industrial premises.

Do you need to spend more of your squeezed budget in a recession year on additional security measures against burglars? If you didn't know the various premises figures, the factories and warehouses burglary trend alone might give a misleading impression of an urgent general need. Again, nothing replaces thorough research but to get around context deficiency you can also ask the general question, "Are there any other figures which would go with these?"

5.3 Sampling and surveys

Excellent textbooks have been written on the subject of statistics for business application but the most pressing question is essentially: "Does the survey sample reflect my intended market?" Only an affirmative response to this question makes sampling results relevant to the identified need for certain information.

Before we go any further, it is useful to think a little about what sampling is and why it is employed. First of all, then, sampling is the selection of a set of individuals from within a defined population in order to gain knowledge or make predictions about the whole of that population. The criteria for definition may be geographical (postcodes or zip codes, political constituencies or historic counties, whole countries) or consist of specified characteristics (income ranges, consumer preferences, ages and so on).

Secondly, sampling is employed to reduce costs and, with limited numbers to address, to speed up the time taken both to gather data and ensure its quality and relevance. There can be something of a trade-off between accuracy and speed but there are systems of weighting data to overcome or at least minimise the effects of such a trade-off.

A key issue in reviews, evaluations, tenders and sales pitches is to ensure that the drawn sample is the same as the target population about which we actually want information. The key response is to spend some time and attention checking the precise characteristics and definitions to guarantee that information is suitable and strong enough for the next stages of project planning.

A summary check list can be drawn up for anyone in business receiving sampling-based reports or contributions which inform wider reviews. It does not assume a detailed knowledge of statistics but will nevertheless enable the user to gain valuable knowledge and assurances.

1. **Sources:**

   - Identify the contact information list(s) which has/have been used (collectively sometimes known as a 'frame'. (This term is not to be confused with a critical thinking term - section 5.5 Framing). These can be of geographical locations or organisations or of databases from which information has been drawn for survey purposes.

   - Check whether the data available has come from specific sampling methods or from lists which provide the required information directly e.g. the local authority's edited electoral register which can be purchased.

   - As for sampling methods, advantages and disadvantages of directly used lists should be identified. The edited electoral register is updated annually but, in terms of target population sampling, it may be limited by the legal right of registered electors to with-hold their details from it.

2. **Sampling method:**

- Confirm the actual method used.
- Seek a summary of strengths and weak-nesses of that particular technique as they apply for your purposes (this should give you further information for making strate-gic decisions). Most methods have straightforward explanations which can also be found by internet search engine if a mar-ket researcher is not available or the report fails to include such discussion in the detail you require.
- Confirm sample sizes are valid for your needs.

3. **Data collation:**

- WOR (WithOut Replacement) – check that the method systematically rules out count-ing the same thing or person twice during one sampling (for example repeat cold call-ing at single occupant home addresses)

- Confirm the method design has not been breached or, if so, adjustment has been made (eg striking out certain entries) and implications fully followed up
- Check the presence/degree of bias introduced by non-responses. There may be gaps in the information through collection failures. Ask what this means for conclusions and recommendations if weighting methods to compensate have not been used.
- Any other influential factors and context worth knowing about?

Internet sampling/polls risk a number of complications which can make them less useful as ready reference sources of information. Firstly, significant potential exists for confusion either through WOR (a single person using multiple e-mail addresses) or non-response (participants may not use some e-mail addresses or open messages only infrequently). There is no easy way of telling which problem dominates a results return.

Secondly, non-response rates may also vary with the offer of incentives, their online uptake and indeed, perception in the minds of potential participants about the appropriateness or desirability of the incentive associated with the survey.

Thirdly, internet polls can draw attention from participants with particularly strong motivations or spare time/opportunity so there is inclusion bias; other relevant fundamental biases, such as gender or race, could be evident based on local factors. Fourthly, a polling website or organisation may be using less than neutral wording for questionnaires (see below). Fifthly, despite the ever-increasing use of the internet, significant groups may be excluded from such a means of contact.

In all of this discussion, the sampling match grid (chapter 4) is a highly relevant tool for assessing the relevance of what is being put forward. On-line research using reputable websites and articles may provide additional information about internet surveys in areas of market interest.

5.4 Information visualisation (IV):

"The error of our eye directs our mind: What error leads must err." **William Shakespeare**

Despite the continuing dominance of the PowerPoint bullet point in business communications, IV has very quickly raised its profile. The key phrase is 'information overload'. The internet provides a literally infinite amount of data and portals for research and advice, all shared instantly and extensively with no more than a couple of clicks of the touchpad.

I read somewhere recently that the internet produces as much information every 48 hours as was generated in the entire history of mankind up until around 2002. Such avalanches of incoming data and sources have to be made manageable for the rather more limited human brain and IV is proposed as an important tool for such a task, turning spread sheet data and commonly occurring words/themes into pictorial representations. The strong visual results are as much artistic as they are managerial, and capture both the eye and the attention by their novelty, patterns and colour.

An IV document undoubtedly has advantages which tempt the executive: the context or overview of the information is instant and has the same immediacy as a communication tool to various levels of management or clients. An IV presentation may be especially helpful to the majority of people who learn by seeing (as any teaching or presentations training textbook points out) and bypasses the problems of text dyslexia. IV methodology expresses complicated comparisons as well as communicates very large quantities of information. It assists hugely in identifying patterns that might otherwise remain unnoticed.

These are formidable points in favour of IV with the danger that it is relied upon to an unwarranted degree as there are still some major disadvantages. Firstly, an IV picture may seem to be straightforward communication but learning theory recognises that people have different ways of understanding knowledge. Those who internalise information best through text and cognitive argument, those who learn and retain through hearing, those with the various combinations of colour blindness and those with processing difficulties for patterns are not going to receive the fullest, clearest communication that an IV-enthusiastic manager thinks they may be sharing by this methodology. The legal framework for disabilities equality could mean that IV may have to be set aside in some of the listed circumstances.

Secondly, in strict terms of critical thinking there is also the risk of decision-making being based on over-processed data. There may be issues of defining groups and batching (section 5.5) prior to formulating the IV image. An IV document is a step removed from the raw figures and options which can be re-checked immediately so it may be difficult to spot omissions. And there may be assumptions of equal value being given to all items or data values when some may be more dubious than others for reasons undisclosed by the IV itself.

It is always important then, to still have the raw data conveniently to hand when being confronted by an IV image. It is possible, for example, to query which rows of spread sheet information have been categorised under which bubbles or words; in short, the general approach of not just accepting the final question and figure for a survey applies also to IV. Only when the background points have been verified can an IV be used as a summary.

5.5 Framing

Now, for a change of gear, think hard about the following question: "When was the last time you came across a charity-sponsored survey which demonstrated there was no longer any problem for that organisation to solve?"

Welcome to the dark art of 'framing', the business equivalent of 'leading the witness' in courtroom dramas. Indeed, 'framing' works on the barrister's principle that you never ask a question to which you do not already know the answer.

Let's consider a little further the charity example above to gain understanding of framing as a persuasion tactic. After all, UK charities at the time of writing receive around £6 billion/year, making them a very large service sector industry. And that is exactly how they approach potential donors.

Broadly speaking, 'framing' surveys adopt one of two approaches: factual ignorance or emotional appeal. Sometimes there can be a mix of the two but one of these strands is usually dominant.

Have you ever noticed how common it is for voluntary sector organisations to start their scripted public interview sessions or questionnaires with phrases like "Are you aware that..." or "Did you know that..." These key phrases should immediately alert the participant to the 'factual ignorance' tactic of being told pre-selected information for a purpose. That purpose is usually to make your agreement with their view in the final question almost inevitable. Such questions can be irritating but can also make any reasonable person feel guilty, ignorant or plain stupid. I would argue that they are used as a form of intellectual pressure on participants to concede the argument, to accept the view that is being put forward *and* to internalise it through the vehicle of painful ignorance.

Concerning the 'emotional appeal 'style of presentation, here is a typical sequence of questions on charity 'survey' forms that drop through the letterbox:

Q1 Do you think there are too many unwanted pets/neglected children/families without clean water today? OR do you think there are more unwanted pets/neglected children/families without clean water than 10 years ago?

Q2   Does this [insert issue fact from Q1] concern you?

Q3   Do you believe that unwanted animals should just be destroyed even if they are perfectly healthy/children should miss out on education and a future simply because they had the ill-luck to be born into poverty?

Q4   Do you agree more money should be spent on [insert issue] as a matter of priority?

Q5   Charity XYZ receives no government funding for its vital work.   Would you be prepared to donate £3 a month to make this service possible?

How could anyone say 'no' to question 9 if they have already said 'yes' to the previous questions? Question 1 is an opinion. There may be deteriorating circumstances but, as crime surveys consistently show, people still believe things were better some years ago even when there are improvements.

Note how question 2 now turns a 'yes' answer to the previous question into a declared personal - internalised - value. And who would not say 'yes' to question 2? Or feel guilty and in a minority if they truthfully answered 'no'? Question 3 continues to internalise with 'do you believe' –

stronger even than 'Do you think'. The question uses emotionally emphatic language.

A more neutral approach would be to quote known figures without editorialising (section 4.4) – and set the number at issue in terms of numbers total animals re-homed and /or in the country, children affected within locally and as a national demographic , and so on. Likewise the use of the words 'just', 'perfectly', 'a future' and 'ill-luck' are examples of editorialising. In Q8 there is the 'lean' – an additional pressure of: 'The government does not fund us – only you (who have said' yes' so far) can help us'.

Such questionnaires are designed to generate an immediate attitude of injustice which borders on outrage and further lessens any resistance to following up a suggested specific action. Again, this directed action is a basic sales tactic recognisable by any business person reading this book. "Sign up to this petition or monthly direct debit if you feel like this", is the closure message – with forms attached to the mailing. For charities this is a very effective way of building guaranteed cash flow quickly, and expanding databases of persons known to be interested and likely to respond positively.

The defence against such carefully constructed questionnaires having their desired effect is the '**Jury Standard**':

ask yourself if the average person on the bus/tube train would really know this or that fact from their daily experience?

If you believe that I have been too cynical in describing the potential effects of framing, then I would like to give you a small research project to follow up in your own time. I do guarantee, however, that this will be the most enjoyable personal development exercise proposed by a business book in years.

Purchase the BBC Yes, Prime Minister Series 1 and pay close attention to 'The Ministerial Broadcast' episode. Here senior civil servant Sir Humphrey Appleby gives junior Bernard a lesson in how to frame survey questions two different ways to get complete completely opposite results. Then take a couple of minutes to compare what is said in the programme script with the questions on the charity 'surveys' that come through your own letterbox.

That wonderful BBC script includes another significant point as a throwaway remark – that only the final question of such a survey is published; all the preceding ones are never mentioned again. The final question is usually presented as a statement of the formula:

85% of the public want/need/support whatever X organisation is doing/demanding

You need to obtain the full survey questionnaire and check for all leading questions which would warp the final results; this precaution is discussed further below.

Particularly with the 'emotional appeal' type surveys, it may well be worth asking what else was distributed alongside the questionnaires in mailings, shown to consumers in High Street promotions or included in the text content/attachments of e-mail circulars. There may be close-ups of faces with big eyes - household pets or young rags-draped children - and cover letters with large type headlines challenging the reader: 'Do you think unwanted animals should be put to sleep/children should sleep on the pavements/have to drink muddy water?' Surely, this is 'framing' even before the responder reads the first question.

And why is this worth mentioning? Because the same presentation principles apply equally to business marketing practices and we can always learn from others. Secondly, this brings us to a more detailed consideration of framing in business.

Many business people read and use information that is published in the mass media as background information for understanding their communities and identifying their markets, innovative opportunities and products. A proportion of that information is produced exactly as described above by organisations which have a vested interest in their services being publicised. Indeed, a primary function of a survey being promoted via press release campaign is specifically to raise profile and make the organisation look like a leading body in that sector. Businesses and individual entrepreneurs use the same tactic with the same agenda, attempting to position themselves as 'corporate celebrity experts'.

General background reading and knowledge picked up via TV, radio, internet or newspapers may be of less value for essential decision-making than might appear at first sight. Again, caution is required.

Any statistics from questionnaires and surveys should be queried by asking, "What is the likely agenda of the commissioning organisation?" and visiting their on-line profiles and web-pages, exactly the same sort of research that every business undertakes when trying to identify prospective clients or partners.

As a minimum practical step, the discerning director or other decision-maker should obtain a full set of the questions contained within the survey. Look for 'leading the witness' phrases such as those given earlier or for anything else that could be suspected of introducing a degree of bias. If there are such signs it is best to just set aside the 'findings' and consider means of identifying alternative reputable sources.

Within the workplace or training environment, it is possible to introduce 'framing' and its guiding effects through a series of discussion questions or statements. A common failure which leads to effective and negative framing is that of **'leader bias'** or **'leader reinforcement'**. A leader can highlight an actual situation being faced by a project team/working group or provide an exercise scenario. They then ask for key ideas, thoughts, feelings and impressions, summary words or skill sets needed.

This approach may seem open and transparent but can prove to be far from neutral and limit the options to be explored. The leader reacts with positive warm tone and open body language (section 9) when whatever they prefer as a 'preferred ' or 'correct' answer is given by one of the attendees. The next run of contributions which follows will imitate the first perceived 'right' answer. The leader's tone and body language can also subtly signal disapproval if a 'wrong' answer is mentioned. Thus a group is both encouraged and deterred simultaneously in order to play a mental version of follow the leader. The final result? A meeting has restricted problem-solving capacity, options are fewer and weaker than might be the case and creativity is stifled.

Support for a project, or resistance to it, can come across as unarguably strong in other ways too, meaning that review is not carried out as thoroughly as it should have been. Assumptions are particularly masked when the project proposal or refusal is accompanied by bland **cover statements** like 'I spoke to Bob and he agreed with this as you can see by his signature'. Such summary sentences miss out an entire indoctrination process – quite possibly unconscious as outlined above - which went on between saying 'Hello' to Bob and his final decision to put pen to paper or left-click his mouse.

Survey figures, it should be noted before we move on, are associated with other areas of concern to critical thinkers. A businessperson may not be looking at results coming from a surveyed general population which resemble their target market and sub-market profiles when s/he really looks in depth at the niche characteristics. (This takes us into the complex world of sampling methodologies which are beyond the remit of this handbook.) There is also the issue of establishing baselines of knowledge and training – giving the facts to people who wouldn't otherwise be aware of what is usual, acceptable or exceptional.

5.6 Batching

This is a very common presentational trick in politics and the media – deliberately grouping together separate categories in order to produce one headline figure which looks impressive. The size of the figure 'demands' a response in line with the actions, priorities and preferences of the presenter. As an example

Proposal to ban X	Absolute number	Percentage
Strongly against ban	250	25
Unsure	300	30
Strongly in favour of ban	450	45

In the above situation, there is a well-publicised proposal to ban X. Someone campaigning against the ban might batch together the 'strongly against' + 'unsure' totals. 250 +300 = 550. Any headline figure is usually given as a percentage only (chapter 4) so the campaigner's lead line will say: "55% do not favour ban". If the percentage is not used immediately the headline will be: "Majority unconvinced by ban proposal".

Someone campaigning in favour of the ban can use the same figures to argue their case. They will batch together the 'Strongly in favour' + 'unsure' totals. 450 + 300 = 750. The headline becomes: "Only 25% against ban" or "75% do not oppose ban". The word version would be "Majority do not oppose ban" or "Majority could accept ban". One set of figures, two combinations and two sets of spin in opposite directions.

A subtle form of batching can be expressed through grouping titles or definitions. Let's say that an organisation produces an internal report with the headline finding that 10% its personnel have faced disciplinary action during the last operational year. However, the definition of disciplinary action actually covers a wide spectrum of misdemeanours: punctuality, personal use of e-mail or internet browsing, loss of memory sticks with unsecured data, anger management concerns assault, What does the picture look like if only 1/20 of that 10% have involved assault or anger management problems and that the vast majority are punctuality or e-mail/internet browsing time issues?

You also have to ask what is being measured when figures are put before you. Is it an opinion rather than a measured fact? This is the prime territory of the hair and beauty products marketing companies. The survey result is expressed as '92% of women say they can see a difference." This is not a direct, data-founded measure of change but an expression of a subjectively perceived difference.

Often these widespread opinion or product surveys combine subjectivity with small sampling numbers. Those numbers appear in the small print which runs along the bottom of the screen or at the bottom of the advert. The much larger headline attracts the attention first and thereby creates a primacy effect of accepting the message. The correction only comes after a strong impression has been made – the equivalent of burying information deep down in paragraphs following survey summary statements and headlines.

Much of the defence rests upon recognising the format or wording of the summary statement, as indicated in the discussion above. It is essential to see the raw data in order to confirm percentages and absolute values, and validity (or risibility) of the sample size.

Batching matters because it can adversely influence business planning. Yet again, examples and figures drawn from background reading/ public domain for planning purposes may prove to be well-worked examples of batching. Undetected, batching creates a strongly misleading impression of a much larger potential support or target market than really exists.

5.7 Ratio Bias

Ratio is a useful summary statistic for businesses but, in assessing an overall situation, we should be aware of a key psychological weakness relating to the presentation of ratio information. The weakness is 'ratio bias': essentially, the bigger the numbers quoted, the greater the significance we attach to it – even if the actual ratio is still the same.

To illustrate, let's say that one research report indicates that 6 units out of 200 of aerosol brand A are defective. Another report finds that 750 units out of 50 000 of aerosol brand B fail to work. Despite the first being 3/100 and the second being 1.5/100, many readers will subconsciously think that B is the less reliable product. This is ratio bias at work.

The existence of ratio bias is a boon to the media for playing up risks – larger numbers are perceived as more dramatic examples to consumers and campaigners. This also means a risk of headlining (section 7.1) and a need for great caution in using reports from the public domain for evidence-gathering in market research or selection.

Of great interest to the commercial environment, the same effect works with the breakdown of figures into time units. A defect product rate of 10 units/day, for example, can seem more manageable than 3650/year altalthough the two are equivalent – and it can be tempting to understate failure rates and trends in this way. The remedy is to standardise all such figures according to operational periods such as VAT quarters or financial year.

It is also true that in meetings, confronted with similar ratios but larger numbers, great significance may be attached to the larger number as described above. As ratio bias is a commonly shared perceptive weakness, then it is likely that everyone present will react in the same way. Even this is only an initial impression it will be harder to overcome than you might expect because of the primacy effect in presentations. In all cases, the remedy is to mention that, "The larger absolute figure might give a strong but wrong impression because in fact the ratios are similar." Next, apply the same units to all ratios involved eg X/1000 or X/year, and show your calculations which lead to the values per unit quantity or time. Only at this point should the preferred choice be introduced.

5.8 The 'compromise'

In strategic review and forward planning meetings of all kinds there are two common variants when it comes to compromise in making final decisions. Both are significantly flawed, and to be avoided. I call them the **true compromise** and the **false compromise**.

The **true compromise** is a genuine and understandably human, if profoundly misplaced, approach: the recommendation to adopt a position or plan which falls midway between several options.

This deficient formula – or a strong element of it, at least – most often appears in group task settings. It is especially likely to show itself towards the end of long, highly detailed meetings when everyone is hot and tired, perhaps frustrated and their usual concentration is failing. A true compromise can also be the outcome of an ill-paced or packed agenda when people are rushing through the later items to beat the clock.

The driving factor to leave the room with a decision at all costs may be a strong fear that there will be difficulties in adhering to project deadlines if there is no conclusion on the day. There may be concern that those excellent ideas which have surfaced so far in the meeting risk being progressively discarded by further meetings. Or that those valuable contributions may come to nothing as enthusiasm and team engagement wane after this one 'big push'.

In such circumstances, the critically thinking attendee may need to encourage participants to get the matter settled with determined thought and paced discussion – but also be prepared to support a second, focused meeting to ensure highest quality decision-making. Across the world, the open plains of business are littered with the bleached bones of failed project planning.

Decision-making time can be reduced by quickly moving to manage participants' expectations; this enables renewed critical thinking to take place. Two points need emphasising:

- A compromise involving anything and everything on the table does not automatically create an effective solution

- Attendees have to be prepared to accept that the 'best outcome' may actually be one out of all the choices (no matter how polarised) or something very close to it

Then the group can move on to identify systematically the pros and cons of the options with evidence-based reasoning to make the decisive selection and structure a plan.

Working methodically in this way makes it clear that there is no favouritism should the concluding assessment or plan come close to one particular option. Or if, after everything I've just said, the final plan does stand equidistant from all the initial options it is also clear that this is not because of time pressures alone. It can be put into action by the participants with confidence.

A last note on true compromise: the basic management principle that people will act most vigorously when they understand just how a position has been reached applies doubly here. Even if time runs out and review has to continue on another occasion despite hideously tight deadlines to get to that position, the enduring quality of team engagement during the project will be worth the effort.

The second variant, **false compromise**, is the result of subtle 'railroading' tactics, used by someone who may be pushing a strong personal agenda or career ambition. The proponent will listen to all other views and note key points and evidence suitable for their particular use. They can then present their own proposal as being a 'reasonable compromise' between all other offered choices.

As social animals, this is a most attractive and pleasantly agreeable option to adopt. It just may not be the right one for the aims and objectives of the company and the project under consideration.

Here, the critical thinker has to respond while facing the disadvantage that the proponent has gained significant goodwill in the meeting room. The reply therefore has be an acknowledgement that the proposal may be a 'reasonable compromise' but that it is not the same as a fully 'reasoned' compromise.

You need to demonstrate that, firstly, the reasons cited by the proponent plus *all* the evidence from other attendees' options can create a contrasting alternative; secondly, that the consequences of the alternative far more closely match the defined aims and objectives of the meeting.

Note that, by this particular approach, you also turn the proponent's broader tactic of generating goodwill against them by highlighting the individual contributions of others around the table towards your final rational offering.

Whether 'true' or 'false', compromise really means 'compromised', and the final dossier might just as well have 'Doomed to Fail' stamped in big red letters across the front cover.

Section 6: Climate Change and Pirate Numbers

Correlation

My attention was recently drawn to a neat and convincing graph which can be found in various places dotted around the internet. Despite news coming from around Somalia and South East Asia, it demonstrates conclusively that since the 1820s there has been a huge drop in the number of pirates worldwide as climate change has kicked in and average global temperatures have risen. The best correlation link I've seen so far is that raised temperatures have driven more pirates to stay on land where there are far more air conditioning units......

Of course, this is nothing but a wonderful spoof but it does make a very serious point which is highly relevant to anyone handling evaluation reports and other feedback. Bluntly put, when confronted with a graph of the general kind: 'as X increases so does Y' or 'as X increases Y decreases, the immediate thought is, "Why does X cause Y to do that?" The actual answer could well be, "It doesn't". This is because we need to distinguish between coincidence, correlation and cause + effect. If we can make this distinction successfully then we do not waste time, effort and, quite possibly, hard earned cash on following up links that do not exist and effects that will never happen.

We do have to be prepared for coincidences in life with no actual links existing whatsoever, despite any apparent patterns. It happens, and the whole subject area of randomness and probability makes up entire university modules and textbooks. Generally, though, this is not an issue in business because if we are looking for feedback or trends for future marketing opportunities and products or services, then we are looking most likely at correlation or cause+effect. So what is the difference between correlation and cause+effect in simple practical terms for business needs?

- **Correlation** has just one key aspect: the relationship between two things or items. Changing one of them ultimately leads to the other one also changing to some expected degree.

- **Cause** has two key aspects: one thing influences another in a predictable way as before. However, additionally, the first thing *is* the reason for the change in the second one. It is the second part which fails the credibility test so often.

6.1 Cause

There are two immediate errors with 'cause' perception which are relevant to business thinking: timing and delayed effect.

Timing: one item is changed consciously, and a second changes during the same specified time period. 'Obviously', altering the first directly leads to the second because those changes have happened simultaneously. Campaigners, directors and managers are all quick to claim credit for having supported the original change and a blizzard of apparently unarguable statistics proves their wisdom. Except....

How do you clarify the situation? The key is to look at the changes to the second item over time beyond the alleged impact period. This is because the figures for that second thing will vary, sometimes rising and sometimes falling. If you have a single intervention and the second item produces an oscillating pattern of gains and losses without any underlying trend in a single direction then you definitely do not have cause and effect. The illusion of cause has been created by a conscious change for item one merely coinciding with an 'up' or 'down' period for the second item. Nothing more. Full stop.

Consider, for example: consumption of salad and fruit (item 1) rises as supermarket availability increases and prices fall during May to July. There is, say, a 10% fall in heart attacks during the same period. Obviously, healthy eating is playing a part with lower cholesterol content in the diet meaning fewer fat-obstructed arteries are finally blocking up altogether. Another small piece of evidence in favour of your five-a-day fruit and vegetable messaging – another contribution to medical knowledge and commercial opportunity.

But, is this right? As advised above, watch the heart attack rates across a much longer period of time and, like many conditions, there will be sharp variations in the numbers of cases. The population diet shift may just have coincided with a temporary fall in numbers.

Yet entire government policies and legislation for businesses – with consequences for profitability – may be bolstered by such failed thinking. Company strategies may be reinforced by this kind of coincidental timing and apparently successful 'sought for' results. And it will be such a waste of time and money without anyone understanding why until the monitoring and evaluation reports belatedly identify item 2 figures as oscillating without an overall up or down trend.

Delayed effect: the second immediate error with adopting a perception of 'cause' is 'delayed effect syndrome'. In effect, if there is a slight timing disparity between altering item 1 and seeing item 2 values change then it is explained away by, "Well, you would expect the intervention to take a bit of time to kick in before we saw results" or similar sentiments. In the mind of the proponent of changing item 1 to achieve particular outcomes, the timing discrepancy merely becomes further evidence that they are right in their decision-making or recommendations.

For the critical thinker in business, however, the response to 'delayed effect' is identical to that for timing. Observe, record and review the item 2 variations over a period of time outside of that used for the claim of direct causality. For both errors, there is also the need to check for context deficiency, asking what is else may be going on during that period that could be relevant?

A particular warning accompanies scrutiny around the two errors of 'cause' perception. We may have a personal bias so that we fail to check the long term trend of item 2 thoroughly or even at all. We are too ready to accept the immediate situation as evidence and perhaps even deem it 'strong' in our own minds and communications. This is 'confirmation bias' in action (section 3.3).

It can be the case that we suppress a personal bias only to succeed in expressing a professional one instead. We may anticipate 'causality' because of other known information about links between the items. Smoking, illegal drugs use, alcohol consumption – all have health issues and consequent legislative and commercial frameworks. So if there is an intervention in any one of these items, we are professionally primed to spot and accept apparent effects as genuine item 2 changes.

Another aspect of poor analytical thinking concerning apparent 'cause' is trying to learn from example. We see a desirable set of figures in one context and simply believe that, by replicating the immediately observable conditions there, we can achieve the same results elsewhere. This is where context deficiency plays a significant role in avoiding a horrible mess.

Let's take an extreme example just to see how false logic of replication works. Annual deaths of motorists, pedestrians and cyclists on motorways are low in absolute numbers. Therefore, according to this kind of conventional 'causal' thinking, we could save lives elsewhere by introducing a uniform 70 mph speed limit across the entire UK road system.

Of course, context deficiency is at its supreme best here. The 'logic' fails to take into account other key facts:

- Pedestrians are banned from motorways. The only people on foot are motorway maintenance workers with all their health and safety precautions deployed, emergency services personnel, again with health and safety protocols to the fore, and stranded motorists who generally stand away from their broken down cars and behind safety barriers lining the route.

- Cyclists are also banned from motorways. The only ones on the motorway are either lost or under the influence of something.

- Motorways have enhanced safety measures: wide, cambered routes; electronic information boards; defined lanes with reflective markers; illuminated signs, junctions and stretches of road; safety lanes (hard shoulders) and layby refuges. Not all these features are found on other types of roads.

Under all these circumstances it is not surprising that death rates are so low compared to other road usage. Knowing this detailed situation makes the original proposition about a UK wide high speed limit seem as ridiculous as it actually is.

The principal lesson, then, about learning from apparent causality and applying the perceived cause to get similar results elsewhere is to research deeply and make no immediate decisions. Context deficiency has to be investigated and removed, and any other, more indirect, associations uncovered. To achieve the latter, we need to have a good understanding of correlation.

6.2 Correlation links – parallel and chain

For some reason, perhaps the simplicity of it, there is often a rush to claim cause+effect which leads straight to instant – and wrong – decision-making. Human nature definitely seems to have a default setting of cause+effect when most observations and commercial possibilities arise as a result of correlation.

Correlation can work as a series of connections or act like a chain of dominoes falling, to change the metaphor. If the changes in Y are desired by someone according to 'supply and demand' economics then each of the links along the way can be a marketing opportunity in itself.

X ----------- A ------------ B ----------- C ----------- Y

Very commonly, however, the correlation explanations work in parallel with several factors separately linking the two observable things:

X ----------- A ----------- Y

X ----------- B ----------- Y

X ----------- C ----------- Y

A recent media report[vii] illustrates this second arrangement, in this case with social policy potentially affecting local businesses. Alcohol Concern's study found that, for every 2 local stores selling drink per 100 000 population, one under-18 person sought hospital admission for alcohol-specific treatment. The report suggested that the government may need to control off-licence (street corner alcohol store) numbers as a consequence.

In this case X = 2 stores/100k and Y = one under-18/100k. Noting that off-licences are the major source of alcohol for young people, explanations for the intermediate links included:

- General availability through greater number of off-licences locally increases the quantity of alcohol at home
- Street shop alcohol sales increases the number of opportunities for under-18s to stand near off-licences and ask legally-entitled adults (over-18s) to buy alcohol on their behalf

These illustrate two very different pathways which make a connection between store numbers and hospital admissions. But there is also an example of the series or chain pattern of connection rather than the 'parallel' explanations. To summarise one of the report's further points in terms of the correlation scheme:

2 stores/100k -------- Alcohol in homes ------- Easy access to friends' supplies ------- U-18 admission

It is also possible that there are other separately-operating link explanations for X and Y which are not listed, usually because further research is needed to confirm their validity: off-licences being concentrated in poorer areas, for instance, where there are also high concentrations of college student accommodation ie a target market which keeps such stores open, local and available also to under-18s.

To summarise then what we have seen so far: two different patterns of links between the two observable things (chain/series and parallel) do not exclude each other as there can be several links of both constituting an overall correlation. You also have to be aware that there could be further links not yet recognised which also create opportunities or raise concerns depending upon your role as a stakeholder in the situation.

This brings us to a couple of very important qualifications concerning what has been said so far. Coincidences happen and they are not usually of interest or application to the commercial world but, having now seen how correlation works through links, we need to be careful in two ways.

6.3 Obscurity

Firstly, there is the problem of obscurity. There may be a credible explanation for a correlation which just does not come to mind readily because it is very specialist and/or requires a type of knowledge outside that of the business sector itself. The average business person either stands very little chance of knowing the key pieces of information or does not think to bring over those facts from an unrelated part of life to make connections.

British media[viii] recently reported some unusual statistics emerging from the last United Kingdom census. There are some apparent correlations between the month of the year in which we are born and the career path we follow. December and January see a high proportion of dentists and doctors; March is the month for pilots; May is fine for political performers (John F Kennedy and Tony Blair); June is the best month to produce a future chief executive. July and August are great for bricklayers. September and October are very good months for doing well academically and at sport – and living longer. By contrast, someone born in March lives 215 days less than if they had been born in October; April babies have higher chances of suffering health problems, demonstrating lower HQs and even becoming sociopathic dictators. Having said all that, and perhaps reflecting the need to be all things to all people by the nature of their work, estate agents tend to be evenly distributed throughout the year.....

At first all this seems little better than traditional astrology or a good 'end of summer' news story before everyone returns to work and the media channels fill up with more startling and significant revelations. But there are possible link explanations and observations that can be guessed and which may remove at least some degree of the mystery.

For example, children born in August may struggle during early years in school when age-based differences in development are greatest. They are at the 'young end' of the school year cohort. However, they can progress with a degree of disadvantage: September-born children are the eldest of their academic cohort and possess a slightly greater developmental maturity which continues through the school and college years.

But there are less obvious facts which may be highly pertinent. Carl Brookes[ix] points out that it is medical research elsewhere which can bring hidden connections to light: spring-born infants are at measurably greater risks of developing a range of significant long term physical and mental illnesses. The link with the months is via the seasons that they cover. The manufacture of vitamin

D in our bodies requires exposure to sunlight; some differences in the health enjoyed by people can relate to their mothers' exposure to sunlight in pregnancy. A subsequent lack of this vitamin for the early developing foetus may have literally life-long consequences through general fitness and school attendance, neurological development and so on.

Interesting though this may be for careers advisors-and presumably for chemists selling vitamin supplements-this example does have wider lessons of principle for the critically thinking business person. It illustrates very effectively the potential obscurity of correlation – the notes above draw together a knowledge of vitamin D and maternal health, school age cohorts and seasons. Not everyone will have such an informed overview and information ready to hand. For the same reason, the business person has to be prepared to research options to find potential explanations and, possibly then, market opportunities or killer facts.

Whilst an apparent correlation can be set aside as a coincidence, that should not mean the same as discarding the possibility entirely. The canny entrepreneur should always be ready to revisit the information if new facts become evident or new expertise becomes available.

6.4 Complexity

The second caution that needs to be understood is the possibility of complexity. A correlation can very easily resemble the proverbial iceberg with 1/9 above the surface of the sea and the other 8/9 submerged and widening out in all directions out of sight. I have already given a hint of just what can lie beneath the surface with the Alcohol Concern study. It features examples of simultaneous parallel and chain/series links; the two types are not mutually exclusive and can be repeated without any limit on numbers.

One method of envisioning a complicated set of links to truly understand a correlation is the Ishikawa or Fishbone diagram (examples easily found by internet search). This kind of diagram brings out the processes very well and can be utilised widely in critical thinking for business beyond its original applications in engineering and industry. The Fishbone diagram, in detailing the multiple chains of correlation links, provides ideas for key interventions to produce an alternative outcome or prevent something from occurring.

To understand the logic of an Ishikawa diagram or similar tool for analytical thinking we can study the structural anatomy of a major disaster: the capsizing of the Herald of Free Enterprise just outside Zeebrugge harbour. There were, in fact, quite a few elements affecting the 'obvious' key factor of high bow waves reaching the still-open bow doors:

Contributory Factor to Sinking: Bow wave rises above open deck level

Element 1 Bow is low in water

Sub-element 1.1 Ballest tanks not adequately emptied before leaving harbour

> 1.1.1 Time pressure
>
> 1.1.2 High capacity pump is unavailable
>
> 1.1.3 High capacity pump considered too expensive

Element 2 Ship increases speed as it leaves harbour

Sub-element 1.1 Master assumes bow doors are closed

> 1.1.1 No view of bow from bridge
>
> 1.1.2 No bow door status indicator on bridge
>
> 1.1.3 No report received that bow door is open

Outcome Water enters decks and ship capsizes.

An alternative identification tool for checking possible correlation links is the '**5 Whys**' technique. Every one of us who is a parent has had the exasperating experience of saying to our children, "Don't touch that!", only to be answered with, "Why?" A whole sequence of one-line ex- explanation and 'Why' then follows, usually ended only by a final heavy "Just leave it alone" or "Because I say so". Complex correlations – and the market opportunities, operations and costs implications or project amendments they can provide – need to be dissected by asking 'Why' repeatedly.

The '5 Whys' management technique is based on the principle that asking 'Why?' five times generally suffices to work back to what can be termed at least a root cause. This is not fixed in stone – it may be useful to ask 'Why?' a sixth time or even more, in order to work backwards towards the true start of the chain.

Effect (problem): My car stands next to my house. The windscreen (windshield) is dirty and needs to be cleaned

Why 1: My car washers don't send jets of water on to my windscreen

Why 2: The wash reservoir is empty

Why 3: All the water is leaking on to the ground

Why 4: The hose between reservoir and washers is de- tached

Why 5: The pump pressure blasts it off the reservoir valve every time the screen washers are switched on

Why 6: The hose rubber has stretched so it fits only loosely

Why 7: The hose has never been replaced despite 113 000 miles of driving in all weathers and road conditions

Cause: This particular perishable item is not part of routine servicing and replacement

Solution: I will replace the hose and check if there is a recommended lifespan for this part

Note that this cause still relates to the original problem of a dirty, dusty windscreen despite all the intermediate steps. The solution is a practical, measurable one. This is because it addresses a cause which, by nature, is a process. That process may be an inadequate one, or it may even be lacking – but even that absence can be documented.

It is also possible to look too deeply, to move on to more abstract notions which do not have such immediate and realistic solutions. We could continue:

Why 8: I know nothing about car engines and maintenance

Why 9: I trained instead as a scientist, manager and teacher/lecturer

Cause: Analytical thinking, strategy and operations fascinate me

This cause is also true – but it doesn't address the problem and get my windscreen clean! We have moved far away from what is a manageable and effective response to a specific issue.

The lesson for business, whatever the method of structured analysis, is a parallel one of due diligence in enquiry when dealing with correlations. Be prepared for some significant effort and don't rely just on the immediate explanations to give a complete picture. It applies especially to interim monitoring, final evaluation, exit cycles and whole project structures/outcomes.

The systematic approach to correlation links of the Ishikawa diagram, 5 Whys and similar techniques does have strengths and weaknesses. It is useful to understand them so that you are best equipped for assessing both the existence and the significance of links which constitute a correlation.

First, the strengths: such techniques enable the practitioner to fully reflect upon, and identify, the intermediate steps or elements. These can be clearly communicated to others for change management, time and motion analyses, project improvement cycles and so forth. Assumptions and failed logic are largely avoided and the abstract set aside in favour of actions which can be subject to SMART objectives and key performance indicators.

The approach also combats a type of objection which is called 'inconsequent or irrelevant argument'. This is a form of distraction (section 10) which is often used more out of heartfelt conviction than of malicious calculation in this type of context. Basically, there is no real link between the conclusion or stance on the one hand, and statements advanced in its support on the other.

In the business sector an inconsequent argument can arise primarily from the punditry management style (section 7) with its fixed ideas which then need to be justified in a discriminatory way and which scorns more analytical input from others. Closely dissecting the situation and identifying concrete causative actions/decisions at each step means that the desired or known outcome is strictly adheres to real explanations rather than to disconnected assertions.

Second, the weaknesses: the techniques work best for those with either a reasonably high level of management experience and insight (strategy) or technical knowledge (operations and change management). This links to a common criticism that the effectiveness of the methods is limited by the abilities of the investigator's current level of competence and formal knowledge. Essentially, it is argued, s/he cannot easily identify those elements, steps or causes which lie outside their experience or general awareness.

In turn, this can lead on to a tendency for inexperienced analysts to stop at intermediate points rather than reach the furthest practical points which can be considered as 'root causes'; a more experienced practitioner is also likely to isolate and draw out more 'root causes' than a beginner.

All the above weaknesses lead to further, potentially significant imperfections: the process is not as scientifically objective as it might appear at first (or even second) sight. The results may not prove to be strictly repeatable – the classic condition required of successful experimental designs. Rather, different people are likely to identify different factors, elements and chains for the same outcome or problem.

Deciding what is or is not a causal element can also depend heavily upon a combination of knowledge and perception about what constitutes events. A flash of lightning and a roll of thunder may be considered separate phenomena by some because of the timing difference or just one event by others since a single electrical discharge is responsible for both light and sound.

They may also subsequently weight different steps with varying, inconsistent degrees of relative importance according to their individual professional backgrounds. This tendency may be helped by the fact that Ishikawa type layouts do not readily identify what lawyers call pre-conditions.

A pre-condition is one which must be in place for the outcome (the 'effect' or 'problem') to occur. Leaving the bow door open for the Herald of Free Enterprise was a pre-condition – if the bow doors were closed, the ship could not have capsized. Increasing the ship's speed upon leaving port, however, was not a pre-condition as it would not have had any importance if the bow doors had been properly secured. Obviously, a precondition is the most important factor or priority to address.

Finally, conclusions by those who have stopped the analysis too early may tend to feature 'insufficient' staffing levels, capitalisation, time/resources allocations or cross-departmental communications. While perhaps true, these are still insufficiently investigated and either remedies or opportunities developed which will cut wastage and take businesses forward.

From all the preceding discussion, there is another absolutely vital point. At the beginning of this chapter we noted that business looks at correlation and cause + effect. Strictly speaking, the latter is actually rare: much of what is called cause + effect is a pattern of obscure or complex correlation linkage just waiting to be uncovered.

For business situations, it may be strongly tempting to accept a direct cause(s)+effect at face value as a simple explanation. Cost implications and the inevitable time pressures on management also encourage a rapid assessment which risks being too shallow. A more studied examination reveals the intermediate steps and elements which give rise to easily communicated action plans, budget costs and ideas for further opportunities; this is an investment of time, not a waste.

Section 7: Degrees of Untruth

Exaggeration and Guesswork

Confusion, bluster and inaccuracy are all natural consequences of the issues raised in this section. Exaggeration, with unrealistic projections, expectations and undeliverable results – makes a mockery of both strategy and evaluation at the two ends of the project management process. Dressing up guesswork as more certain than the situation or conclusion really merits can be equally disastrous if it is accepted at face value. Speculation is a prime example of this kind of managerial minefield.

It also raises the question of who you can trust to be effective and accurate; some are most definitely more trustworthy than others when you understand how they come to their recommendations and see their track record. A study of punditry equips the business participant with some essential perspectives on leadership and decision-making.

7.1 Headlining

Headlining derives its existence from the journalistic practice of providing a truly dramatic top line which creates an exaggerated impression of the more measured facts and phrases which follow much further down the column and in much smaller print. In this way basic information is inflated by one means or another to generate an interpretation which is disproportionate to the situation being described.

The immediate impression of deep crisis or amazing success is not justified to the same extreme degree by the details upon examination. This can go unquestioned because, even if the size of the discrepancy is perceived, office politics or emotional overtones accompanying the subject may deter objections. No-one wishes to be perceived as heartless in sensitive matters but this should not crush intelligent consideration of a true situation.

Any report or sales pitch, especially verbal ones and/or delivered in the heat of the moment, may provide examples of this form of manipulative behaviour. It has also been said in political circles that legislative bills before Parliament carry titles that are the opposite of the actual contents. Critics have argued that the Freedom of Information Act devoted many of its paragraphs to restrictions of access!

Let's just see how it works for a fictional headline that numbers of British tourists with a tick-borne tropical disease have shot up 50% in just five years. When we look at the figures behind the headline it turns out that such 18 people were admitted to hospitals in 2011. The figure for 2006 was 12.

How much of the increase in absolute terms also reflects the rising population here in the UK over the last ten years, and the proportion of population travelling to the disease zone? Context deficiency is therefore also an element of the headlining impact (section 3); we can further note in passing that the dramatic presentation is made possible by quoting percentages in the headline without the accompanying absolute numbers appearing immediately alongside them (section 4).

The danger for business and political communities is that such headlining practices (especially when linked with context deficiency) give an impression of far more decisive action and greater possible results than may well be delivered. It encourages people to anticipate further trends or opportunities which are just not going to materialise. What is being pushed is, in reality, too little in absolute terms and therefore inconsequential or ineffectively slow-acting for whatever change is needed or for markets to develop.

7.2 Perception versus Calculation

'Perception versus Calculation' or PvC concerns an initial statistic presented in positive tones which emphasise how large a figure it really is. It is only when the reader or listener sits down with a calculator that they realise the given figure is not going to make much impact after all. This is because they work out that the much vaunted sum is actually tiny compared to the size of the problem or relevant budget.

Perhaps, unsurprisingly, a very common occurrence of PvC is the announcement by a government agency or corporation of how much it is spending on an issue. This can be featured as an uncritical headline in a politically favourable newspaper; it is made more dramatic and effective because, at the same time, relevant background figures which would reveal the pathetic inadequacy of the investment are not provided (again, the sin of context deficiency – section 3).

A large element in PvC is **intentional psychological deceit**, taking advantage of the gap between the everyday experiences of most people with their modest household budgets and the national balance sheet figures which are of a totally different order of magnitude. One recent example of PvC is that, against a background of rebalancing the UK national budget deficit, the incumbent government declared its policies were successfully saving the hard-pressed UK taxpayer around £500 000/hour. To a teacher earning less than £20/hour or many workers on around £8/hour this is a huge sum compared to their income. And that is exactly what the purveyors of PvC are counting on to create an impression of significant fiscal competence.

The response is to counter the headlining and PvC by uncovering relevant information and placing it alongside the original headline statistic. In the above example of 'spin', the figure required to provide the background for a realistic assessment is the total UK government income. For 2011-12, the same tax year in which the savings figure was announced, the government receipts are expected to reach £589 billion or **£1.6 billion per day**.

We can go on to standardise the figures just to make the point completely unambiguous: £500 000/hour = £12 million savings per day (£0.5 million x 24 hours). The budget anticipates £1.6 billion income every day. Given the universal adoption now of a billion as meaning a thousand million then the savings are roughly 1/49 000 of income. Put another way, if you had around £49 000 annual salary and managed to save £1, just how impressed do you think your bank manager would be?

Another classic example of PvC would be the past promise by a government agency to spend £300 million for childcare across five years, with the claim that it would make possible 1 million new places and mobilise the potential of the national workforce. But the headline statistic of £300 million actually worked out at £1.15 per child per week – hardly such a decisive level of funding that it would cause parents to rearrange their work lives and private childcare providers to re-write their business plans. If you are an entrepreneur or company seeking contracts, PvC-type announcements from agencies and blue-chip companies need hard scrutiny.

PvC can work the opposite way, too. Large financial commitments can be disguised as small sums by reducing them to daily rates. This technique is commonly used in sales of all kinds which involve subscriptions and direct debits, and involving cash flows in presentations. In this case the context deficiency is a comparison of estimated pricings or advantageous terms and conditions provided by rivals. There is still a need to respond to this form of PvC by scaling up the daily or other cost rate to, for example, an annual budget figure which is more meaningful for planning and projections. Even 'just 50p' per day works out as £182.50 in a single year.

Marketing for charity appeals and commercial subscriptions (including many life assurances/funeral plans) are based on this **reverse PvC** principle. The intention is to provide the tipping point for a sell by making the costs look like a bargain, or at least reasonably affordable. Thus, without truly counting the cost, you find yourself paying ahead of your actual demise with a funeral plan, providing various insurance company reps with a decent standard of living and wondering exactly how you ended up adopting an African aardvark.

7.3 Relative Frequency

The term 'relative frequency' is not found often in reports and articles but its practical vocabulary is common, manifesting itself in journalistic phrases such as 'twice as likely...' or 'triple the risk of...'. However, a potential problem which creates a dramatic but misleading impression lies behind the use of 'relative frequency'.

Let's say that a review in a business magazine, think tank economic review or the like determines that someone living and working in London 'twice as likely' to apply for a flagship start-up loan scheme than someone based in Birmingham. However, if we look at the actual figures, expressed as "number of applying entrepreneurs/1000 registered self-employed", what might we find? London

= 12/1000 and Birmingham = 6/1000. So the 'twice as likely' comes down to a difference of 6/10 000 adults. The difference in standardised figures hardly leaves you with heart palpitations over going bankrupt if you are in the West Midlands.

The comparison might be further refined using a match grid (profile characteristics of different groups or professions falling into insolvency, for example) which would yield further valuable information and, possibly, different figures. However, the overall point remains that there is a consistency in application rates across parts of the United Kingdom which is observable even if it might be counter-intuitive from all we see of London's economic robustness during difficult times. And isn't the point of critical thinking in business to avoid assumptions?

Ask for figures in terms of per 1k, per 10k or per 100k whenever confronted with a summary "You are three times more likely to...." or similar in any document or presentation. Again, as elsewhere, it is always worth asking why the absolute numbers have not been provided in the first place; the response and the demeanour during the answer to that question will say something about the firm or staff with whom you are dealing.

Returning to our example, we need to understand the wider context of what may be at stake. Such analysis doesn't just ruin dramatic stories by robbing them of attention-grabbing headlines. Uncovered findings can also be catalysts for planning: the above illustration might encourage reflection, for example, on deployment of resources and contracts for business competence courses and personal debt counselling services, for regional development strategies and positive marketing messages versus negative perceptions. It is more than just an idle curiosity of analytical thinking.

7.4 Speculation

Here, the term 'speculation' does not refer to wilder flights of fancy or to investments in stocks and shares. It has a narrower meaning in critical thinking, being a proposition or series of propositions, not based on established fact, that lead to a conclusion which is itself uncertain.

This form of argument is a favourite of conspiracy theorists everywhere but it makes its appearance in the real world of business too. Speculation may be easier to spot than some other forms of dangerously slack thinking because of its format as we shall see in a moment. However, be warned: somehow it has a compelling force all of its own which can sweep all logic before it.

The structure of a speculative argument commonly follows a sequence along the lines of:

"It is highly likely that X will increase in these circumstances; in turn, this means Y will probably diminish and therefore Z is almost certainly going to look like........."

But notice those key qualifying phrases: 'highly likely', 'probably' and 'almost certainly'. It is not what they have in common that is important but what they do not have. And what they do not have is certainty. There is no guarantee at any stage before the conclusion is pronounced, so the question then arises as to how realistic is that final assertion. There is a cumulative degree of uncertainty which becomes a significant risk to any planning which counts on 'Z looking like.....' for its success.

Therein lies the danger for the unwary who are swept along by the sequence of logical steps without considering the existence of possibilities and probabilities along the way.

Let's put these giveaway phrases under the microscope: firstly, they indicate that each of the phrases within the argument is really an assumption. We have already seen the significance of assumptions – and, above all, the need to avoid them – in chapter 2.

Secondly, how have these intermediate assertions been tested? How does the proposer know that something is 'highly likely' or 'probable' or 'almost certain'? What methods and indicators have they deployed for each of the phrases to confirm that they are describing reality? Actually, it is not unreasonable to take one step back and ask if the phrases have been tested in any way at all for their validity and consequences.

Thirdly, the astute reader will also have noticed the intrusion of quantitative vagueness (section 3) by the use of 'highly likely' and its literary cousins. Where there are no absolute measures and figures for the various stages of the speculation, and the wording therefore represents a best guess, we have already seen the dangers when the same word means different things quantitatively to different people, even within the same projects team.

The fact that there is less than absolute certainty being expressed implies the existence of other alternative chains of events and conclusions or consequences. Can these other consequences be identified as we work through each phase? What is the final range of outcomes – and how many of them are detrimental to the health of the project or entire business? Can any of these alternative outcomes become suitable catalysts for practical actions which are provably more beneficial than those points which have already been argued so dubiously?

In short, speculation raises far more questions than it answers with its final statement. That is what the listener should be doing – asking awkward questions along the lines just mentioned. After all, it is ultimately the responsibility of the proposer to fully justify their position and proposals with completely valid means.

Having suggested at the beginning of this section that speculation is not too difficult to spot I would like to highlight one important qualification. Sometimes a speculative argument can turn up disguised under a cloak of **fake absolute certainty**. The tone of rock-solid dependability of the argument and conclusion is achieved through the use of the word 'will' or 'obviously'. Let's return to the example formula but this time insert 'will':

"X will increase in these circumstances; in turn, this means Y will diminish and therefore Z will look like......"

The first defence here is the general wisdom that the more steps there are involved in a process, the greater the likelihood that something will go wrong. This is in itself a perfectly valid basis for questioning the apparently cast-iron guarantee provided by the conclusion. After all, it is rare for anything to be easy or straightforward in the business world. However, the disciplined critical thinking response is the same as for the more uncertain expression of the argument – question in detail the justification for each and every stage of the argument being presented in this way. Hesitations and inadequate answers by the presenter will provide all the necessary warning signs you need.

There is another twist to speculation, particularly in those presentations which seek to persuade rather than merely to inform their audience. That is the use of the word 'obviously' as in the statement: "Obviously this means the moon is made of green cheese". "Obviously" is the alarm bell of critical thinking!

There are two elements to the deployment of this word – **framing** and behavioural psychology. The framing element is that the word leads the reader or hearer in one particular direction only. No option other than the one stated is acknowledged, let alone explored and assessed. Again, this must be challenged immediately and I return to the key point that it is the responsibility of the proposer to completely justify their position using valid means. Questions need to be asked. Why is it 'obviously'? What is the basis for such certainty? What are the options? How have they been assessed and why are they inferior and to be discarded in favour of this single choice?

The problem, though, is that we are human – and group dynamics comes into play. There is a well-documented phenomenon called '**pluralistic ignorance**' in behavioural psychology. What it means in practice for this business context is that everyone is afraid of admitting that they might not know why an assertion is 'obviously' so. Each attender assumes that everyone else present understands completely some rationale unknown to him/her why the word 'obviously' has been used. No-one dares to ask essential questions because they are afraid of making an idiot of themselves. Thus a spectacularly bold and possibly unjustifiable statement or idea goes unchallenged and untested; grief and costly consequences come later down the line.

Let's now return to the original formula for speculative argument for another cautionary observation:

"It is highly likely that X will increase in these circumstances; in turn, this means Y will probably diminish and therefore Z is almost certainly going to look like........."

During an overlong review meeting or sales pitch attendees may find their thoughts drifting towards unrelated matters such as reducing the golf handicap, the perfect holiday, the post-work shopping list or outstanding DIY tasks for the weekend. It is particularly easy in this state of mind to miss out the body of the presentation, focus on the concluding sentence in isolation and consider the work done. It does require mental discipline as well as strong coffee to follow the issue in detail when speculative argument is involved.

There is no simple formula for an appropriate response here – the golden rule is to question every point that precedes the conclusion so that the latter, a significant recommendation perhaps, does not simply slip by default into the 'to be actioned' list.

In this respect, then, the primary defence is very similar to that of framing in surveys; the very last step and its resulting headline statistic cannot ever be treated in isolation from the process that brings it about.

7.5 Punditry

A major story during the last few months has been the downgrading of European and USA credit ratings by the Standard & Poor's Agency. But is the whole world listening to the wrong people? The situation reminds me of all those ex-players and managers on the weekend sports programmes. These football pundits seem to spend quite a bit of time after a game explaining in no uncertain terms why certain features and incidents were inevitable.

They just happened to say the opposite in pre-match expectations earlier in the day.....

Credit ratings are significant at national or international level of decision-making but board and project management meetings, partners around the table in the law firm offices, editorial review sessions, business seminars, tutorials and professional development classes, sales teams get-togethers, cross-departmental working groups, webinar question times and even informal gatherings around the water cooler and kitchen kettle – all such gatherings have one thing in common. Or, more precisely, they have one type of person in common: the pundit.

Such meetings are usually, by their very nature, venues for strong, competing and confident voices. Collectively they constitute the natural habitat of the 'pundit' and the 'seer'. The pundit, like his or her namesake on television, radio and internet streaming, fairly consistently gets things wrong but always somehow seems to survive the debacle professionally to proclaim further erroneous judgements. The seer, on the other hand, anticipates and predicts with a record of success that Nostradamus himself would envy.

It is vital to discern which of these characters has influence in the workplace, especially as forceful personality can win out against quietly argued points. Critical thinkers just cannot afford to ignore such a powerful factor in strategic overview, prioritisation and decision-making.

So then, let us turn our attention to the two classes of thinkers just mentioned, pundits and seers, and familiarise ourselves with an important series of contrasts. Ultimately, it becomes apparent from this series that what recognised or self-proclaimed experts think is far less important to businesses, their staff and profit margins than how they think things through.

The pundit typically has just a single overarching 'concept', approach or values structure. It is a coat hanger (CH) viewpoint or understanding upon which everything else – assertions, data and processes - is hung. This CH and its corollary thoughts are held with a total degree of certainty and exclusivity. There is no room for researching facts, forming ideas, and deeply understanding issues. The seer, however, characteristically can accept any number of concepts or proposals rather than focus and hold tightly on to just one; issues are to be investigated, according to the seer's approach to challenges, consciously 'mined' for what can be developed into future actions.

The decision-making process which follows on directly from this one key difference in thinking can be very unsubtle in its effects on a company's growth strategies, team effectiveness and resources consumption.

The pundit has total confidence in their CH, as the start and end point for any situation assessment. Indeed, they do not see their CH as an outlook, but treat it more as a 'known fact'. This makes it very easy for the pundit to dismiss any opposing views. It also means that critical thinking is neither valued for its role in decision-making nor employed.

Instead, the pundit will disregard or play down any measurable evidence which contradicts their CH or the direction where the CH leads in arguments and conclusions. However, attention to detail is selective; retaining the CH with supreme confidence also allows the pundit to embrace the smallest detail or most tentatively ventured view which bolsters their position. This aspect of punditry is an extreme form of confirmation bias which is discussed elsewhere. That is the decision-making process against which any form of analytical thinking competes.

The seer, by way of contrast, doubts that there are ever single and simple answers to situations they confront. As a consequence, they tend to gather facts and suggestions; they consider competing views as having merit and will be familiar with preparing lists of pros and cons.

The seer will be flexible, embracing far more than just those propositions and pieces of information that happen to strengthen their own starting position. The seer integrates critical thinking as a basic and immediate assessment tool for conducting their deliberations.

That last point hints at another key difference between pundits and seers – the process of putting together a justification for final decisions and actions. For the pundit, this is very straightforward as they produce assertions and conclusions based directly on the CH and very little else.

At best, any consultation will involve providing opportunities for people to forward only anything which is consistent with the CH. There is an effective censorship in place which staff may self-impose, knowing that contributing material or thought is usually futile. At worst, statements are merely delivered and declared from on high without any input at all. The business seer, however, sets up some sort of procedure which funnels varied facts and ideas from a range of contributors. These processes will involve review stages and active, self-critical teamwork; listening, not rejection, is the pro-active characteristic of decision-making.

The final result is that the pundit releases a simple declaration with a tone of certainty and closure. There is a single, solid conclusion with no further debate. The seer proves far more flexible, using the varied information and sources (shared with colleagues) to provide a list of reasoned priorities and preferences; the list itself and its underlying rationale may remain open to further amendment.

The number one characteristic of whatever the pundit determines is always 'clarity'. There is no ambiguity about the content of the message and the firmness of its deliverer; staff will know exactly where they stand in relationship to the proposed idea or action. They will not be expected to deviate from the set action plan and anything unforeseen will have to be reported back to the pundit for their sole consideration.

In contrast, the number one characteristic of a conclusion by a seer is 'appropriateness', accompanied by justifications and possible options to address flexibly any unknown future issues. Staff will have a degree of freedom to exercise individual or task group judgment on the nature of responses and practical actions.

And a final observation: the CH may be closely associated, in the mind of the pundit at least, with their personal identity, ego and/or outward projection of professional competence, aspects which go beyond the confirmation bias mentioned earlier and deep into the territory of self-verification. The seer has far fewer problems of self-identity and external worth, enabling them to access the valuable information and insights contributed by others.

All this does mean that defensiveness and emotional intelligence have an overlapping role with any analytical reflection whenever the management meeting pundit stands up to speak. And everyone else in the room will know it. Where the pundit is at work, there the staff turnover may be highest, with all the cost implications and loss of competitive efficiency that follow.

7.6 Plural numbers

One very simple form of 'over-the-top' presentation concerns the use of plural numbers. An early sales report may refer to 'scores' of newly-launched units being sold. Closer questioning then reveals that the number of sales is 43 ie two score and three. This reflects a common practice in journalism which will also say, for example, 'dozens' when there are 25 people involved. Basically, the headline of "scores, or dozens or tens of X "creates an impression of figures which are greater than the reality.

The example above is more likely to turn up in verbal deliveries and ad hoc notes. In written form, there is a similar exaggerated impression created through more subtle means when reporting values. The difference between 'quarter of a million' and '250 000' is one of association with a much larger number (million) versus a straightforward figure.

The appropriate response here is to keep repeating the actual figure, encouraging full attention to precise data. The tactic also fosters a sense of honesty which contrasts with the longer worded exaggeration. In this sense, the repetition is a form of softening up the attendees to accept the number-based conclusion.

If the report or speaker persists with the exaggeration by association with the larger quantity, then it is reasonable to point out firmly what is happening and require the use of explicit numbers. In the case of written material, the reviewer can make written corrections, insisting on the unadorned statistic each and every time it occurs. At the very least it will send a no-nonsense message about standards of precision which are desirable.

The last comment is perhaps a suitable conclusion for this section. Disparate though the causes of degrees of untruth may be, they all result in a need for real clarity to improve both decision-making and presentational honesty.

Section 8: Heart of the Matter

Emotions

Emotions make up the second side of the critical thinking Quantity, Emotion and Processes model which was introduced way back in section 2. In this section and the following one we will take a look at ways in which emotions can confuse clear thinking and damage profit margins. Technical issues and protocol problems in management are often easier to address than personal clashes between subordinates or even senior management, and the consequent balance of decisions can really suffer. Middle managers struggle to handle the frustration of watching reasoned arguments being dismissed almost instantly in favour of personal preferences and prejudices. And entrepreneurs may have no-one available to argue more objectively against their personal misperceptions about how popular their latest idea or invention will prove in the marketplace.

8.1 Overtones

We can start to make sense of what can be a messy subject by first looking at the language used in making a case. In particular, emotional overtones associated with words can affect the emphasis and direction of a presentation in ways similar to framing (section 5).

Marketing and sales teams have particular skills as wordsmiths and it therefore never hurts to ask yourself when a word or phrase seems particularly striking why exactly that should be so. Does it emphasise a point, exaggerate its importance, clarify or feed a prejudicial assumption?

Many words do carry overtones – additional messages which provide an emphasis or a leading in a particular direction through the emotional reaction they generate. And they can reflect strongly held personal positions. The classic illustration is the quote by writer Gerald Seymour in his novel Harry's Game: "One man's terrorist is another man's freedom fighter." This is such a powerful truth. The polarisation it summarises has very practical outcomes in politics and, inevitably, commerce and business opportunities in a global economy.

Pro-life and abortion rights campaigners can be recognised instantly by their vocabulary, using 'baby' and 'foetus' respectively to describe the same unborn being. In order to remove the inevitable emotional clouding around debates and policies, terms such as 'potential life' have to be used in order to clarify rationales for public policy, health services and social entitlements.

Across the western world the terms 'obese' and 'overweight' are significant in more than one way. Both are legitimate medical terms with medical definitions based on Body Mass Index and other measures. Overweight is not as severe as obese in strict medical terms. However, 'overweight' carries a far less judgemental overtone than does 'obese'. Whatever the clinical realities, 'obese' carries a strong notion of personal indiscipline regarding diet and exercise. It can be argued that the media, advertising, dieting, sports and activities and personal training industries all have a profitable commercial interest in exploiting this nuance.

Another common aspect of overtones comes with '**comparison by association**'. Typically, this takes the form of saying something along the lines of, "Our manufacturing sector output is now below that of [insert small country with incompetent or disdavantaged image]". It is a way of emphasising extremely poor performance which makes for compelling communication. However, it is a calculated and seriously misleading form of exaggeration. The response is to point out that 'comparison by association' makes for a dramatic picture with strong emotional overtones but does not provide a practical analysis.

Recognising the tremendous power of emotional overtones and association, there have been conscious attempts in a number of fields to develop neutral terms to avoid emotional reactions, stigma and prejudice. The word 'leper' has been discouraged officially since the 1960s. A replacement term like' leprosy –affected' makes the point that the disease does not define a person's identity; it also underlines the fact that direct consequences such as loss of income can cause distress not just to the infected person but also to family members.

There is similar thinking behind phrases like 'Person Living With HIV'. This cautious approach is a good frame of reference for preparing a neutral account when confronted with a less than objective project pitch or report.

During and after the recent 2011 UK-wide riots there was a lot of debate over the terms used to describe those taking part in the violence and looting. Relatively neutral words such as 'theft' were not much in evidence, 'rioter' seemed inadequate for the level of looting and robbery, and some media outlets were criticised for using the milder term 'protester'.

Stronger labels conveying disapproval and reflecting the degree of criminality abounded in the media: 'scum', 'thugs', 'hooligans', 'mindless yobs' and 'terrorists' is a sample list of the widespread condemnation. Although the word 'criminal' was used early on, it was certainly a minority choice. Interestingly, this more neutral term with less emotional overtones came to the fore only after the anarchy was stopped and hundreds of people started to come before the courts to be judged in a more rational, detached way.

The **personal element** usually bases itself on direct experience. The term 'terrorist' for the riots might have seemed surprising and excessive. However, the United Nations' definition of terrorism consists of: "acts....designed to create a state of terror in the minds of a particular group of people or the public as a whole for political or social ends". Those caught up in the anarchy, intimidation and even occasional death during the recent UK city riots would certainly argue that this described precisely what they had lived through. The word 'terrorist' would not be at the extreme end of the vocabulary spectrum as far as they would be concerned but instead would be deemed as highly appropriate to their own experience.

It may be helpful for critical thinking to consider the idea of terms being located somewhere along an **emotional spectrum**. Smack – hit – beat could, for instance, be seen as the range of terms which are used in debates about corporal punishment for exactly the same physical action. The full range reflects a move from a single restrained punishment to harder and repeated force. 'Beat' carries the additional implication of a level of out of control violence which equates to criminal action.

Similarly, slim – thin – skinny has been under scrutiny for the size zero image of models and linkage to anorexia and self-perceptions/self-esteem of young magazine readers.

The concept of an emotional spectrum is a very practical one for advertising and, indeed, for business ethics (clothing sizes and body type aspirations as part of the multi-billion global fashion markets are recent examples). It is also a tool for distinguishing between fact and persuasion when handling strategic recommendations arising from reviews, expert evidence and the highly personal areas of performance appraisals.

Whatever the topic, we are faced with the challenge of determining where along the range a term is justified for the particular situation we face and this always has a subjective personal element.

8.2 Personal subjectivity

This influential factor is a huge self-challenge to achieving analytical objectivity. We do need to recognise that it is deeply embedded in each one of us and goes beyond the perceptions arising from personal experience, as mentioned in the previous section. Personal subjectivity is indicated by the type of language we all apply to ourselves, especially in the areas of negotiations and decision-making.

"I am firm" has a positive overtone, a virtue of knowing our own mind. "You are obstinate" or "You are stubborn" carry negative overtones of disapproval, an unjustified refusal to change. We all have this dual perspective which we apply to ourselves and to others. We also unconsciously link this perception to the value of others' arguments and information, even when we use other reasons verbally to rationalise our own position. And we (choose to) forget that the person on the other side is doing exactly the same.

As an illustration of how difficult it is to be objective as human beings, we only have to look at the failures of current hate crime law. Legislation currently includes the notion that anyone feeling 'insulted' or 'distressed' by the words of others can allege the incident is driven by hatred. It was originally intended to tackle blatant antisocial behaviour.

Instead there have been wrongful arrests, dropped prosecutions and settlements out of court as a result of personal reactions – ultimately innocent victims of complaints have included several street preachers, hotel owners, a teenager with a placard and a group of animal rights campaigners protesting against seal culling using 'offensive and distressing' cuddly toys dyed red....

This degree of sensitivity might seem both ridiculous and irrelevant for the hard -nosed business sector but there is usually a weak point or two of such proportions within each one of us. It is a question of being able to recognise such vulnerabilities and using self-knowledge or emotional intelligence as an additional tool of calm analytical thinking.

This brings us to the practical question of how to respond to emotional overtones. The points and arguments should be restated using the most neutral words and phrases which can be chosen. Ideally, all this should be written down along with any clarifying questions which arise. In order to do this, a strongly developed self-awareness is always important. Acknowledging this analytical vulnerability exists is the most important defence against being swayed.

Someone once said: "Challenge everything – especially what you agree with". Absolutely right.

8.3 Softening up

This is rather different to what has gone before in this chapter. It is less about the actual words used as the projection of a particular attitude + calculated presentation. There is a spectrum of emotional engagement in softening up techniques ranging from 'exclusive to you' (generate sense of privilege and/or sympathetic engagement) through taking advantage of thought patterns (associated emotions reduce the analytical scrutiny and increase acceptance) to primary engagement of emotions (gain a heart-led practical response).

We'll work our way along this emotional engagement spectrum, starting with the lowest end of engagement. This end tends to be where the emotional effect is a mild degree of panic pressure as the offer is 'special but you have to take it now or lose it forever'.

The **'Deal or No Deal'** sales technique consists of initially proposing a high price or limited features of a package, then progressively reducing the price and/or increasing the benefits to a low level. This can be accompanied by 'friendship' signals, either verbally or through body language cues (section 9). It can be usually linked to an 'on the day' or very short period deadline for acceptance.

The overall idea is that you are receiving special consideration – and a really good deal. This approach differs from applying usual discounts for repeat custom or bulk orders or early invoice settlement by several orders of magnitude.

Traditionally, variations on softening up have been a lead tactic for face-to-face sales in sectors such as timeshares or double glazing but some of the 'mechanics' transfer into business-to-business dealings. A part of a timeshare process can be to ask the punter how much they think the luxury apartment or villa will cost to hire for a week; any overestimate is met with an emphasis on the proposed price. This has the effect of making the large upfront bill seem more reasonable but if the punter still hesitates a more limited offer with less cash up front is still immediately available.

I once sat through an hour-long double glazing presentation at home; the price was progressively reduced to only one third of the original starting point – even then it was exactly the same as a non-reduced quote from another firm. The last point is a key one: whenever there is an experience of softening up then comparative data from elsewhere is invaluable. It not only confirms the reasonableness or otherwise of the cost, terms and conditions on offer but also reveals much about the company making the sale.

'Now or never' softening up has also been effectively adapted for the digital age with the exploitation of e-mail newsletters and website/social media postings. The sales process has a progressively changing price scale but this time it goes in the opposite direction to the example above. A lower initial price for a service or goods is quoted, along with a short deadline for purchase. After the specified date passes, the price rises significantly.

If the service on offer is a workshop, for example, then there is the additional imperative of places being limited; the same may apply to goods or workshops. Bonuses abound – pdfs, interactives, video clips and series, DVD's and books. All these are intended to provide a tipping point for a buy-in decision. The softening up principle continues to be applied because the workshop, webinar or other contact offer introduces other services or goods or joint ventures - classic upsell.

The response is to ask if/how much is needed? Are there free/low cost sources or alternative tenders? Careful calculations can judge value and costs rather than accepting softening up figures and the artificial pace of imposed deadlines. It can sometimes be hard to remember that the deadline is someone else's choice but not yours.

'**How you say it**' moves us further along the emotional engagement spectrum. This second technique of softening up applies to strategic argument and project planning as well as sales pitches. Here, the tactic is to use a sequence of phrases or assertions early on that coincide with the thought patterns and verbal expressions used by the targeted individuals in meetings. It is a calculated exploitation of the listeners' confirmation bias, in effect, using strong emotions associated with those patterns and expressions to bypass the critical scrutiny of the receiver.

Success with using easily accepted statements can be measured by observing listeners' postures, head nods and smiles, and so on. Only after this point has been reached and the meeting is in a more receptive state of mind is the more doubtful proposition with weaker supporting evidence put forward.

Just knowing that this approach can exist in even supposedly more critical surroundings such as boardroom meetings is an important defence against being swayed unduly by it. Being prepared to reject an assertion after receiving one after another easily accepted statement is key.

We should also be on our guard against the softening up statements. Just because they may be used to soften up ahead of delivering the dubious proposition does not make them right either. Each one has to be analysed on its own merits and preferably before moving on to the next one. This prevents the softening-up sequence from being deployed.

In doing so, we have to be wary about the long association – literally a lifetime in development and reinforcement - between thoughts and our emotions. That association is always a weak link in our critical thinking armour.

'In Your Face' is a third type of softening up which is found at the far end of the emotional engagement spectrum. It intentionally engages the emotions as the primary means of generating a looked-for response. Seeing suffering directly leads so many people to set up charities or other not-for-profit organisations, particularly when the victim of the disease or calamity has been a loved family member or close friend.

I have to admit that my most powerful arguments for people to part with their cash to medicines for leprosy- or HIV-infected people did not involve figures. I used A2 blow-up pictures of the faces of patients before and after receiving a course of tablets for a few months.

I simply told the story of the patients while the audience stared directly into the eyes of those whose health had been regained so quickly and dramatically. People were so astonished by these changes- and affected by the personal stories – that a positive response was guaranteed, immediate and relatively lucrative. People were relating to people through these pictures, and not to clever words, unarguable logic or fascinating statistics.

 In the charity sector, the ideal photograph for a fundraising appeal would be a little girl with wide eyes and in a pitiable state of dress looking straight to camera while cuddling a cute puppy with floppy ears and panting grin! Keep a quick score of all the charity appeals that feature on TV adverts or turn up as circulars and e-mailings and I am confident that what has just been written will barely seem an exaggeration ...

The heart response is intended to lead directly to a lucrative commercial response. This is also the principle behind the sustained support for football (soccer) club shops, for example. Not many people, in other contexts, would walk down the street in early summer wearing a bright scarf or a gigantic foam hand. And consumer resistance to the infamously high cost of replica shirts is often overcome by fanatical dedication to the team as much as the effective nagging power of offspring.

8.4 Anger

The display of this emotion and associated behaviours can be subject to misconduct proceedings in the workplace and can fracture working relationships. Anger management courses make a great deal of business sense as a worthwhile investment as anger itself detracts significantly from an individual's ability to be open-minded. It can also be true of a meeting cohort such as a working group which feels that it is no longer being listened to and/or is being bypassed and feels frustrated.

When listening to a statement an individual or group may hear something that arouses a very strong negative reaction. If early on, then the anger may well create a strong 'blanket refusal' to accept any part of the following argument, no matter how well researched and constructed. A reaction later on may lead to a limited acceptance of what has been shared up until the point of upset. Whatever the timing, any open frame of mind which had been originally present for selecting best options will have been lost. If truth be told, the open mind may only have been slightly ajar – the trigger for the angry response might be a legitimate challenge to a prejudiced view or assumption or a long-held company cultural value.

It is reasonable to guess that rising irritation might be shown by a proposer as others focus repeatedly on a weak point of a business case and press for further information or clarity. However, that scenario is different the calculated strategies which are intended to induce a strong re-reaction.

Another aspect of anger, then, is the specific debating tactic of keeping calm yet **provoking an opponent** so that, upset and disconcerted, they present their case less coherently and effectively than would otherwise have been the case. Of course, the aim is to damage the credibility of their argument by the results and overall impression created by the evident ill-temper.

Certain forms of temperament manipulation can really upset even the most mild-mannered proponent and undermine their evidence or rationale in meetings: using a patronising voice tone and dismissive body language (turning the body away while talking or 'talk to the hand' and dismissive gestures). Insolence or disrespect can be expressed through mocking humour or barbed sarcasm.

Breaking a sequence in presentation by repeated interruptions on small or irrelevant points is a more subtle but equally unpleasant form of manipulation. Here, the manipulator can cause damage yet seem to mean well by what they are doing. Not only do they successfully irritate the presenter, and decrease the credibility of the original proposal with the loss of temper, they may even gain credibility for their opposing assertions. After all, they seem to be genuinely engaged with the original proposal rather than being negative or destructive.

An awareness that the provocation tactic exists, and the main techniques for fulfilling it, is a remedy in itself. The moment that any of the above methods can be identified, caution and a determination to remain calm should be uppermost in the mind.

Self-control need not be strictly defensive in order to keep the actual issue at the centre of analysis and discussion. After several such attempts to provoke, it may be reasonable to dispassionately contrast your own measured demeanour and concentration on essential facts with the behaviour of the opponent, expressing disappointment that subject under discussion is not being considered perhaps as carefully as it should be.

This sort of response or comment is best delivered in a calm and confident tone, with non-targeted eye contact glancing around the room and accompanied by appropriately relaxed body language (arms resting on table, body relaxed in chair). It is then clear that you are not stating this out of pique and rising irritation. Such a detached manner gains influence within the meeting or sympathy with an audience, and isolates someone who is obviously trying too hard to be upsetting.

As elsewhere, body language and tone, psychology and communication theory are all tools to clear the ground in which the critical thinking can be planted, take root and flourish.

8.5 Prejudice

"Prejudice is never easy unless it can pass itself off for reason" **William Hazlitt**

"Few of us ever take the time to check our brains as long as our prejudices are in working order" **Anonymous**

Prejudice is more of an attitude than a tactic: the person believes that they are defending a position or putting forward an assertion on purely rational grounds. Beneath this rational veneer, however, there are often emotional attachments or particular experiences which determine the stance in question and make convincing counter-argument next to impossible. (The links may be obscure even to the person who is demonstrating the prejudice.)

The person may react with anger to the internal conflict and frustration which is generated when the prejudicial view is being successfully challenged with 'difficult to dismiss' facts and statements. In business management terms, prejudice creates inflexibility, with set plans and avoidance behaviour if factual challenges become too threatening to the perceived truth and a defined comfort zone of activities.

Because of the highly personal and internalised justifications for prejudicial attitudes, **anecdotal evidence** features strongly alongside confirmation bias. Dependency on anecdotes means that large amounts of data are overlooked in favour of what has been encountered directly. The '**vividness effect**' of anecdotes, always a strong influence on more open minds, is hugely significant in reinforcing a preconception.

Certainly, the variety of media platforms and their editorial biases now give ample opportunities for constructing fears and strengthening a certain worldview. One example may be the discrepancy between actual crime levels and perceived likelihood of becoming a victim. That gap can be explained in part by this sort of effect.

For businesses, the practical response has to be one of detailed research. In one area a while ago, the closures of large factories led to a loss of 24 000 jobs. The overwhelming anecdotal evidence came in the form of a myriad of headlines and personal stories, generating a sense of great loss. The region was, apparently, a manufacturing desert.

Yet during the same period, over 20 000 new manufacturing jobs were created in the same region, mostly at small companies. The vividness of the headlines, pictures and columns disguised the limitations of the damage and existence of new business to business opportunities.

At the very least, the vividness effect may mean that there can be marketing opportunities for customers willing to pay for services to respond to their perceptions. Arguably, the insecurity about crime may provide some additional income advantages for the various personal security industries.

But that kind of perception distortion does no favour whatsoever for the individual member of the departmental steering group, board, management team or other decision-making body of which they are a member.

In terms of critical thinking, you have to deal with any inclination to the dramatic or even offensive, calmly and factually. You also must respond ruthlessly, not moving on to the next point until all persons present (with the possible isolated example of the prejudiced person) have acknowledged the validity of whatever evidence has been offered. One must resist the temptation to jump stages and instead ensure that everyone has had the chance to weigh all the available facts before judging.

The power of individual experience over extensive sampling has to be challenged directly. While conceding an instance as recounted in anecdotal evidence can be valid, it is only a small part of a larger story. Demonstrate the inadequacy of the offered anecdotal evidence as 'typical' of the full situation by using as much data as can be obtained.

The prejudiced person will only rarely change their mindset so the overall strategy is twofold: firstly, to isolate their evidence as incomplete and unfit for purpose and, secondly, to isolate the person from the decision-making process as far as possible by appealing in rational and commercially acceptable terms to an overruling majority or senior line manager.

8.6 Sound bites and slogans

Sound bites and other simple slogans have been mentioned earlier as a form of omission in argument. They may seem profoundly truthful and focused but in reality all they do is inhibit engagement with all the complications of planning, evaluation, strategic overview and consequent budget prioritisations. They skip several stages of argument because of in-built assumptions, and avoid all the scrutiny that would normally accompany each separate stage. They can be perfect vehicles for sharing prejudices.

Shallow thinking might not manifest itself just through verbal slogans and written summary statements in a business meeting. Some of the tactics and errors we have discussed earlier in the book may also be associated with the 'canned quote' approach: quantitative vagueness, citing averages or cause + effect. The quick summary fails to reflect a complex reality and all the analysis associated with that situation.

A prejudiced person thus has several means by which single dimensional thinking and argument can be projected. An apparently strong collective case can be created by expressing a single slogan in a package of different ways:

- make a sound bite headline

- use a back-up average statistic

- follow with a quantitatively vague assertion based on that statistic (or even seem reasonable by using 'many' without further data)

- finish with another summary slogan which parallels the first

And the reason why the argument is 'effective'? We, the recipients, fail to challenge the biased view or argument because we tend to accept such shallow thinking more easily than a correct but detailed analysis. We prefer simplicity to complexity. If this were not true, then the slogan-driven advertising industry would not exist as we know it.

Again, it is helpful to be forewarned about shallow thinking and the 'packaged prejudice' business case outline above. Yet we still have to be on the alert for our own analytical self-discipline to be slipping. This caution is especially true when the prejudiced view chimes with some part of our own wider outlook or experience as highlighted elsewhere in the book under 'confirmation bias'. We can really betray our own analytical attempts when we feel the strong emotions associated with particular life events, memories and perceptions of those around us in earlier times.

It is also frankly realistic to acknowledge we also accept shallow assertions more readily when the issues affect our wealth, well-being and comfortable lifestyle or standard of living. Anything which threatens these important parts of our lives will be scrutinised for injustices and failings of all kinds far more readily than anything which protects and enhances our comfort, resources and status.

Challenge everything then – especially what you agree with.

With those warnings bluntly spelt out, how can a critical thinker respond to the prejudiced view point? The answer is to confront what the prejudiced person deems 'obvious' and dissemble the complexity underneath their summary statement or sound bite. Use factual evidence as much as possible, demonstrate correlation links in detail and quantify different sub groups and stakeholder roles.

If the information is not readily available, it is possible to indicate that additional data is needed and sketch out some of the complications. Offer further research and review, and seek adjournment of the discussion to delay decision-making until later.

A critique is insufficient: provide positive alternative recommendations in detail based closely on data and conclusions. Do not merely reject the one view and its limited options for action as it is the development of positive answers which will win over meetings.

As recommended elsewhere, all this should be carried out calmly and with relaxed body language in order to defuse any confrontational aspects and create a more open atmosphere. The overall counter-approach should be that the plan, issue or assessment is more complicated than the proponent has indicated; the presentation needs the attendant support of personnel management skills to achieve both the immediate strategic challenge and a desirable long-term cultural change.

Section 9: CONfidence?

Non-Verbal and Status Arguments

"I can watch myself and my actions, just like an outsider." **Ann Frank**

There is a real challenge to analytical thinking which relates less to the quality of factual information, logic or the structure of argument than to an attitude of confidence. The attitude is communicated with reinforcing expressions of body language, tone, speech pattern and so on. Confident assertions can also be undergirded by appeals to expertise or status – prestige arguments – or expressed repeatedly with a rock-solid firmness unsullied by self-doubt.

It is worthwhile having a basic understanding of such powerful means of messaging. The critical thinker is then better equipped to carefully deconstruct and analyse what is being argued or reported without distraction. This is not easy to achieve because there are many means – some of them really powerful but still operating at a sub-conscious level –by which the body and mind can make statements.

As human beings we place a great reliance on non-verbal communication. Should the non-verbal message contradict the verbal one then, as a general rule, humans ignore the verbal content and accept the non-verbal persuasion. We are up to four times as likely to remember a non-verbal message as to recall any words that are being spoken.

9.1 Positive image projection

At job interview training it is emphasised that impressions formed within the first 30 seconds of entering a room can also be some of the most lasting ones. It is also harder to change such impressions once they have been made than to present a positive image in the first place. In the business environment it is possible for someone to project a strong initial image from the start and, despite spouting drivel, still win the day.

There is something else worth remembering if you are on the receiving end of a major face-to-face presentation: the person on the other side may have had professional training in non-verbal communication to improve their chances of career success at your company's expense.

A positive image projection can cover verbal cues other than the language itself (pitch, tone and vocal fillers) and also strongly features body language (posture, facial expression, eye contact and distraction behaviour). We need to take a little time to examine each of these in order to build up a realistic picture of why such a firm and disciplined mind set is required of business people if they are to avoid being taken in.

Voice pitch is a tool of anyone required to project confidence professionally. The general principle is that a higher pitch reduces the credibility of what is being said. Margaret Thatcher deepened her voice for her landslide 1979 elections and afterwards. Again, analysis is required of the content not the 'packaging element' of the delivery, and deep pitch should not be allowed to convince us of shaky arguments.

There is a further, related aspect: positive image projection includes training to manipulate **the speed of speech**, again to provide another subtext which complements the sense of the sentences being articulated. Margaret Thatcher very successfully combined lower pitch with a slower delivery rate to convey an outstanding degree of gravitas.

This is particularly applicable when under pressure-the speaker may be aware from   audience responses that the information being shared is not being accepted. A trained and experienced presenter will ensure that the delivery rate continues at the calculated speed. In contrast an inexperienced presenter will speed up to the point of nearly incoherent gabbling as nerves take their toll on the mind. Analytical thinking is the opposite of the preacher's note in the margin of his sermon script: "Argument weak here – speak faster, shout louder".

By itself, someone's **tone of voice** provides almost infinite confusion for analytical consideration. The professionally trained communicator consciously utilises a warm tone which conveys approval of what they themselves are saying as well as serving to establish links and agreement with negotiators from the other side.

This presents a significant dilemma if you try to take an interpretive cue from the tone: a naturally confident salesperson, for example, will also project warmth unconsciously and genuinely. But such a convincing tone of voice can also be counterfeited as a basic acting technique as noted so how do you know what are you facing? The answer is the oft-repeated one on these pages – to side-step any decision-making which can be influenced by tone and return to the quality and completeness of the content.

A flat tone might simply indicate jet lag or too much late night 'networking' at the hotel bar prior to the task at hand; but such a tone can also betray disapproval or disagreement with what is being delivered. If the tone changes from one section to another then that can indicate the area of review or sales pitch which may merit closer investigation.

Vocal fillers are repeated words or short phrases such as 'Okay?', 'You know', 'Like', 'And Stuff'. They can also include sounds, classically 'Um' and 'Er'. They are discussed further below as they can give away a lack of confidence in the message being delivered. For our purposes here, though, we simply note that a trained or naturally confident speaker has these vocal fillers largely removed from their professional or public communications. This creates a smooth presentation flow which in turn reinforces an impression of compelling, argument being shared by an authoritative and competent person.

Concerning posture, an **open stance** conveys high confidence in the facts and messages, conclusions and justification for the case being made. Common instances of open stance include the speaker coming out from behind the speaker's lectern or table at the front, or sitting with legs extended and not crossed ie knees and feet apart. Honesty is implied by gestures such as open hands, palms outwards, appealing to the group or audience.

An open posture also apparently makes someone seem more likeable as well as more confident than someone demonstrating 'self-protective' postures such as crossed arms; the argument or plan is better received from a more liked person at a subconscious level, and therefore possibly less systematically scrutinized.

One manipulative selling tactic is to consciously use '**postural echo**' in 1-2-1 meetings for gaining acceptance first for the person and then for the idea. Postural echo means adopting the same posture as the other person to whom they seem to be listening closely, indicating they are thinking similarly; it is very much seen as a bonding phenomenon which occurs unconsciously. A strongly confident person, however, will not mirror others and this has the effect of looking objective when giving information and ideas whatever their merits or logic.

Similarly, any **nervous gestures** or agitated behaviour (fiddling with rings, for example) – like overall posture - can be controlled through training and their direct relevance is not as a tool for judging truthfulness. Rather, their absence has a key effect on the generation of a positive image with a strong effect of raising the proponent's credibility in the opinion of the viewer.

Body position and movements are not the only significant subtle messengers. **Facial expression**, as might be guessed, can also be a factor in communication. Basic biological facts support this idea: *Homo sapiens* has more face muscles than any other species and we are wired for near-instant communication through 'reading' faces.

Usefully, many basic facial expressions mean the same wherever you find yourself on planet Earth but you may have to consult locally about expressions with particular meanings or nuances. The risk of misunderstanding is obviously increased in this global marketplace of multi-national companies linked through computer-based digital video. Even when the facial expressions are identical, cultural factors and values may mean that, for instance, anger or concerns through stress are not shown in business meetings, legal conferences or public forums. But the reaction – and the consequences for clear analytical thinking – may still be there in private.

One aspect of facial expression which is particularly influential is **eye contact**. It is really potent and, unconsciously, provides the basis of many of our judgements about others. It is helps structure verbal exchanges as it provides cues and assurances about listening. Maintained at the end of, say, a situation briefing, eye-contact serves as an invitation to now speak for the other meeting attendee(s) with which it is shared.

Failure to make eye contact as a regular pattern can lead to breaks in conversation flow with – from our point of view – a less comfortable negotiating experience and negative impression of the other participant. That risks overruling the merits of the content of discussion, or excessively downplaying them.

Similarly imperfect thinking can result from the capacity of eye contact for emotional communication. Dilated pupils can register in the brain of the person sharing their argument – and elicit a positive response of 'liking' further – without that person being aware of this type of interaction even taking place. This creates a situation in which both the speaker and the listener are providing positive encouragement to an idea in a feedback cycle. It can mean that the level of scrutiny falls and poor quality critique results. This is one explanation of why two people or a small group sometimes have a seemingly 'amazing idea' which – although apparently thought-through at the time to the satisfaction of all involved - does not stand up to careful examination by others later.

9.2 Prestige

"That [the atomic bomb] is the biggest fool thing we have ever done. The bomb will never go off, and I speak as an expert in explosives." - **Admiral William Leahy**

Prestige is a major distraction tool utilised in decision-making from national government policy down in everyday life. It is also the refuge of the 'Do as I say – don't think about what I'm telling you' business brigade and can be a powerful means of projecting confidence and re-inforcement. Prestige is essentially an appeal to some external factor or resource in order to gain attention and strong credibility for the views being put forward.

One very effective use of prestige involves highlighting **qualifications or technical background** so that the presenter is considered an expert. In this way, the argument is already 90% won-after all, who would dare to contradict someone who specialises in the area under discussion? If rejection happens at all, then it is more likely to take place on the basis of other factors such as budget priorities or practical resources/personnel available and so on. However, we do need to look at the issue more closely because all is not as it may seem and immediate, automatic acceptance is neither inevitable nor wise.

If the choice of options is being directed primarily by a formally qualified person, in business you still have to ask just how relevant those qualifications are to the particular project or proposal in question. With business-specific qualifications the situation may not be as clear cut. It is, for example, possible to have gained a qualification with a variety of modules; some of these subjects may relate to what is on the table and others may be irrelevant.

The issue therefore is to clarify, usually through direct questions, exactly what links exist between the project under discussion and the nature of the certificate held/course completed by the person arguing the case. It is essential to separate valid judgement by an appropriately qualified individual from unjustified demand to be believed without further scrutiny or the contributions of others.

Of course, formal academic or vocational qualifications are good general indications of a general intelligence and an ability to learn which is transferable – all usually demonstrated by a successful work record. There are large numbers of senior managers on high tax band salaries who first joined companies with college rather than university qualifications and/or as temporary staff but have progressed through skills, continuing professional development, experience and personal determination. They are experts in their fields but may not always have the degree certificates to prove it.

The message is the same regarding issues of qualifications and experience: whatever the status, listen to what is being said or reported, bringing critical thinking skills to bear in the usual way as described throughout this book. And this includes testing with more than one source as an additional check to strengthen confidence in the evidence base.

There are variations on the issue of prestige, 'association' and 'testimonials' which are common in the business sector. Basically, it is patronage by another name – and, ideally, that other name is a famous one. And if we in business are not influenced by testimonials then why do we put such a special premium on collecting them for website profiles and other marketing and sales? Or on the covers of our books? Or use as introductions to new prospects?

An association or testimonial serves as a first stage criterion for selecting those to whom we might listen. This can be positive as long as we also maintain the healthy and systematic caution of analytical approach to their work and opinions, and keep open the option of involving others.

The prestige concept can also be one which can be practised subliminally in various ways. Association with **ostentatious wealth** is one such method of messaging: "I am rich because I know what I am doing" and "So many people are prepared to pay for my [high] quality expertise that I accumulate all this money". I saw a promotional video recently for an entrepreneur business advisor and one of the first shots featured an expensive car. The video message was nothing to do with vehicles but the implication of "This way to wealth" was clear.

The mind is wired to take in far more visual information than we are consciously aware of so favourable impressions generated by wealth cues can sneak under our guard. Systematic consideration of the content without assuming prestige derives from competence can offset the psychological disadvantages of such unconscious reception.

However, visual tactics may not be the only means of subliminally messaging. The same authoritative impression can be generated by the deliberate, extensive use of **technical terms** or other impressively long words and phrases which leave the hearer feeling confused or inadequate for understanding what is being presented. Either way, there is an internal pressure since the hearer's options seem unpalatable – admit an apparent intellectual inferiority (confusion) or confess poor knowledge of the project/ inability to relate specialist advice to the issues (inadequacy).

There is, though, another choice to these forms of apparent professional suicide. Ask the provider to avoid technical terms and use straightforward phrasing early on during the meeting for the convenience of the whole group and for those beyond the walls who will also use the information eventually. This ensures effective communication across the organisation so it is a positive move anyway. It does place pressure on the provider to explain anything complex in an understandable way, shifting the focus back on to the quality of information.

9.3 Repetition

Repetition is a basic principle of propaganda, a crude trick but one which is highly effective and consistently used in politics of both the parliamentary and office kind. In practice it is the equivalent of hitting the discerning mind with a blunt instrument. A single summary statement is repeated as often as possible within the meeting or organisation until it is readily accepted by the majority of people, especially those with a key role in subsequent decision-making and budget control. It turns what is at best an untested assumption into the unquestioned – and unquestionable – truth. . Repetition is a tactic which is particularly favoured by the pundit in business meetings.

Linked to repetition is the dark art of writing the **sound bites and slogans** which facilitate the process of mass memorisation and acceptance, plus skills in delivering them. This is a whole subject in itself which is beyond the scope of this book. However, understanding that contemporary culture places great emphasis on deploying this sort of skill is fundamental to being forewarned in business.

Just to give one brief cameo of techniques involved, politicians and company PR staff are formally trained not to pause for breath in the middle of a key explanation. This prevents television and radio producers from cutting out part of the message that the interviewee wants to deliver, and so the whole is broadcast.

A special word of warning is appropriate here regarding **internet sourcing** to back up arguments. This is a particular form of repetition. A proposer could seek support for their position by reviewing internet-based sources and drawing up an extensive list of sites which provide the same information.

There are two complications: firstly, just because something is said on the internet is no guarantee of factual accuracy. Indeed, a huge amount of the supposed 'information' and 'data' presented on the internet is inaccurate for one reason or another. Secondly, many websites, forums and blogs borrow 'information' and 'stated facts' from one another. If one statement is untruthful, that doesn't stop it going around the world in seconds and being repeated a myriad of times. In effect, it recreates repetition as a propaganda effect.

'Everyone knows', for example, that the Great Wall of China is the only man-made structure which can be seen from space. This is commonly mentioned on a host of sites. And it is a total myth – the Great Wall of China is still too small to be seen from that lofty vantage point. So 'Everyone' is wrong. The same role of repetition can also be achieved with re-tweets, further magnifying the potential for misleading repetition to have a psychological effect through social network platforms.

There is another aspect to this perception of '**credibility through attitude**'. It is perfectly true and has already been heavily emphasised that you set aside the confident attitude of the proposer order to carefully deconstruct and analyse what is being argued or reported. As noted earlier, this is not necessarily an easy thing to achieve.

Equally difficult, however, the competent analytical thinker also has to give all the time and attention which is required to scrutinise fairly the information and arguments which are presented by an unconfident speaker or writer. Critical thinkers try to be objective in approaching anything put before us but we are still human and occasionally fail. So then, we need to be on our guard here as much against ourselves as against the external source of information.

Unbidden, a very strong link indeed quickly forges itself in the mind when the ear and eye are assailed by hesitations and silences, verbal breaks like ums and errs, tentative and defensive postures (hiding behind tables, having arms held across the body or legs crossed instead of an open stance), lack of eye contact with the listeners, nervously gabbling fast or mumbling into papers held in front of the face.

The best long-term solution is, of course, some kind of presentation training for the messenger but that doesn't deal with the here and now. An immediate practical response, as far as effective decision-making is concerned, is to diligently write down the points being made as they are being delivered, stripping the data and argument of the distracting behaviour and poor expression. In this way, any merit in what is being said will be more readily uncovered and carefully analysed.

We can wrap up this chapter by repeating the summary theme now that you have worked through the reasons which lie behind it. A confident person – natural pundit or trained salesperson – will not give out some sort of simple, instantly recognisable sign that blatantly contradicts the position they are promoting. There is no straightforward equivalent of the apocryphal advert in the local newspaper:

LOST: dog with three legs, blind in left eye, missing right ear and tail broken. Answers to the name of 'Lucky'

Whether through passionately held belief or systematic training, positive image projection is a powerful potential spoiler when it comes to careful analysis. Be prepared to be particularly rigorous and assertive concerning the quality of the material, logic and options placed in front of you.

Section 10: Shifting Ground

Changing the Argument

In this section we examine ways in which arguments can mislead by 'morphing' – phrases, meanings or data alter from the starting position according to the needs of the proposer's next statement. The receiver has to be alert to such changes in order to re-state the issue or proposal in its original terms and focus clearly and exclusively on the initial intent. Then the alterations can be dealt with one by one, highlighting the changes and what they mean to the strength of the argument.

Some of the means by which elements of arguments can change are subtle and not necessarily intentional. They may just reflect the general slackness of analytical thought in everyday life or result almost inevitably from the uncritical bludgeon of the pundit approach to management.

Others can be calculated by the presenter to the point of ruthlessness for the sake of getting their own way at any cost. Sometimes it is hard to distinguish the underlying attitude or motive but office diplomacy and good customer relations usually demands that the recipient assumes

slackness rather than slyness on the part of the protago-
nist.

10.1 Toning down

The first instance of shifting ground is 'toning down'. The
proposer advocates an initially simplistic or extreme
view/action. When it is successfully questioned and
thrown into doubt, the proposer unhesitatingly moves on
to a more moderate second position.

Toning down has a great advantage to the proposer, prov-
ing a useful tool for the determined but amoral self-
publicist seeking celebrity expert status and a competitive
edge. It has the effect of creating an image which is un-
conventional, imaginative and truly worthy of all other
similar adjectives that accompany the pioneering 'lone
thinker'.

The extreme statement seems to come from someone
who dares to say what others – at best – dare only to
think. It makes this one person seem to be ahead or at
least outside, of the crowd. In short, they are a leader, a
guru, of conceptual free will. Then the moderate statement allows the same person to look reasonable,
pragmatic, in touch with the realities of the business sector they are addressing. The movement in position
therefore draws less criticism than might be expected.

There are elements of punditry in this tactic and it certainly is a tactic for self-promotion out of the ranks of the 'ordinary' people. Nevertheless, and despite the introduction above, slipping from an initially extreme but indefensible position to a more moderate, well-evidenced position is quite often seen in ordinary discourse and problem solving.

Ideally, the recipient is free to point out the change in position, the gap between the two positions, and the factual weaknesses which make the extreme starting point completely untenable. Even the moderate stance can be similarly dissected.

In practice – and particularly when facing a proposer who is skilled with humour or confident charm – the recipient can seem pedantic, bureaucratic and depressingly humourless. While being totally in the right, they lose the sympathy and good will of the audience. And the argument is lost with very little else being said. It requires measured words, gentleness and an injection of a matching dose of humour or charm in return to avoid such consequences.

Have you ever emerged, shocked and bewildered, from a management meeting or sales negotiation asking yourself, "The issues and pros and cons were so clear, but the worst option has just won out. What just happened?"

Toning down or some variation of it may just have been launched as an ultimate weapon of "mass distraction", taking out all opposition in one blast of brazen eloquence and winsome personality.

Critical thinking has to recognise the power of the 'being human' element as well as the investigative processes, and the effective response here definitely requires such understanding.

If this seems to be making mountains out of molehills, it is worth remembering a relevant point of social psychology. Once an impression is created, it can be hard for people to re-orientate their perception. Far better that the image perception of the 'tone shifter' is dealt with as quickly and determinedly as possible otherwise you could be facing many more such meetings and painful outcomes in the future. It's even worse if the CEO or line manager develops a favourable view of the 'tone shifter' as the 'go to' person – the celebrity expert or pundit mentioned elsewhere. You will really have to battle to gain a hearing, let alone success, any time from that day forward.

10.2 Changing definition

Parallel to the notion of 'toning down' – a shift from an extreme to a moderate, negotiable position – is the second type of 'moving target'. This is moving the meaning of a term or definition of an object/idea during a discussion. This may be deliberately in order to achieve a parparticular conclusion decided in advance or, again, it may just be unintentionally ill-disciplined thinking. The development of the case, plan, pitch or review subtly alters towards the conclusion favoured by the proposer unless challenged.

The most effective way to challenge – and not a bad practical exercise anyway – is to note how key terms are being used at each step of the unfolding justification for a preferred decision. Next, referring to the list in front of you, check that there is a consistent definition or function. If so, then assess the logic and reality of the presentation using the responses indicated throughout this book.

If not, then review out loud by reading the list, using digital projector, shared documents or good old flipchart – whatever is needed so that everyone understands at the same time that the definitions have drifted and before decision-making progresses any further.

They will need to understand:

- there is a problem (a series of changes of definition which move away from original usage)

- what are the consequences of the changing definitions (how the argument is warped and led in a particular direction)
- the cost implications of this misleading usage (so no-one thinks you are just being a nit-picking, fussy member of the awkward squad)

You can then return to the starting definition or usage of a word/term and build the counter argument. Never demolish without constructing afterwards. At each step where the definition changed, contrast the gap between what your plans project and what the original presentation asserted.

Slightly ruthless, perhaps, but the notion of changing definitions, why they matter and how much a resulting corrupted decision could cost can be quite subtle. Remember, we use such tactics habitually in everyday conversation so we are geared to exploiting rather than shunning this poor quality of argument .

A final practical comment here: it is easier to keep track of changing definitions during the delivery of formal presentations and reviews of one kind or another. But they can occur spontaneously – and be more difficult to recognise and list – in the back and forth exchanges of question/answer panels or other verbal sparring. Here, two or more people may each offer their own slightly different understanding of a term with their own in-built assumptions. The result is confusion and 'going round in circles' rather than a clear direction towards one particular conclusion. The lack of intent or calculation does not make the mess any easier to clear up.

If you have input or influence, then post-session write-up of contemporary notes is probably the most useful answer. Lay out the different positions or get participants to restate then pick up the differences. Ask panellists to provide comment and explanation before final circulation to all attendees. This is both courtesy and good leadership management.

There are positive effects arising from a changing definition: it is always possible that a term will change in an attempt to avoid emotional overtones and the appearance of promoting the views of one side only. More neutral terms can reflect function - a description of role. During the period of writing this book, the conflict in Libya continued to feature on the front pages and websites of the major newspapers. It has been interesting to see how the term 'Rebels' alternated with 'Fighters loyal to the National Transition Council'. 'Rebels' is a term with disapproval overtones which reinforces the view of the armed forces and administration that remain loyal to the previously governing Gaddafi regime. The longer term

'Fighters etc etc...' reflects a functional truth without conveying a particular viewpoint on the situation.

A particularly tricky variation of changing definition is that of naming countries and regions. Of great interest to multinationals and local joint venture partners, maps need careful scrutiny and referral. South Sudan, for example, with its oil production potential, gained an independent geopolitical identity in July 2011. On-line maps were only just being changed two months later.

It is always possible to wander carelessly into significant territorial disputes or regional associations which can make or break market potentials: India/Pakistan borders, the histories of Tibet, Taiwan and China, the emotional and geopolitical realities of Israel/Palestine, the African international alliances associated with mineral-rich but peace-deprived Democratic Republic of Congo; the respective oil production and refining capacities of South Sudan and northern Khartoum-led Sudan. The list goes on....

Regional identities and markets may relate more to the distribution of ethnic groups or infrastructure limitations in Africa and parts of Asia; ethnic populations may have both 'outside' names and local language names; terminology needs to be monitored carefully in order to ensure that the same populations and districts are being discussed by everyone present. The definition of population in terms of demographics and geographical distribution is otherwise vulnerable to confusion, and project development runs the risk of misplaced investment.

The last comment provides a link to another type of shifting definition which affects multinational or interregional feedback. The definition which changes may not be a word or term but the method of assessment or information gathering applied in each country or region.

Be aware that a definition can change over time, and that it can become a like-with-like (section 4) or batching (section 5) issue. One example – with consequences for personal security product businesses and support marketing companies – is that of UK violent crime.

The categorisation of crimes as 'violent' altered with effect from April 2002. Before that date, local police themselves decided whether or not an incident was actually a violent crime. From April 2002 onwards, an alleged victim decided if they perceived what they had experienced as a violent incident, and the police then had to classify it accordingly. In practice, previous examples of violent crime such as assault were now grouped with general public order offences and harassment (including being sworn at with no personal contact) and violent crime numbers apparently soared.

The aims are laudable: to get a better picture of actual police workload and public perceptions and experiences. However, the new and broader definition of violence means that any comparison of pre- and post- April 2002 statistics is invalid. This has never stopped politicians quoting rises and falls according to expediency and there is a risk or temptation for researchers and sales teams to do something similar where changed parameters are involved. Inappropriate actions may result from powerful but wrong impressions.

The defence is not just to identify sources where there is a huge difference and/or a long period of time involved. Request brief notes and clarifications on actual definitions *and* data-gathering techniques since the two can be connected. Having identified such a significant change in practical definition (or different combination of groups for batching), a response will incorporate several aspects:

- A statement that the comparison is invalid **and** that any created impression needs to be set aside
- A re-statement of definitions or batches
- An emphasis on the differences and what they mean for the data and decisions involved
- A request for like-with-like (can completing a match grid)

- A new schedule for decision-making once data has been established on a like-with-like basis

10.3 Distraction

Here, the primary issue under discussion is left behind as a proponent raises other points which have only a tenuous or broad subject link to that topic, and which cannot prove the validity of the original assertions.

A worthwhile exercise is to go to one of the news channel or business magazine websites and look at the comments sections under major stories. You will very quickly notice that the correspondents veer away from the primary argument or idea, and raise side issues, irrelevant new points or personal experiences with varying degrees of connection to the initial subject. We have all lived through management meetings with similar content and lack of structured thought!

What is also depressing to observe is how often – and quickly - contributions degenerate from a factual focus into sweeping character assassinations and personal abuse, an extreme form of the unacceptable practice of rubbishing the witness (see below).

Other questions and side issues crop up quite readily – distraction is a very common flawed tactic during open discussion in meetings, although it can turn up in reviews and strategy reports.

The tactic of distraction away from the initial focus is utilised when, under difficult and detailed questioning about the primary issue, the proponent wants to avoid conceding the argument or case. Distraction may also reflect the subjects with which the speaker is most comfortable.

Within the business sector, distraction may also be used by someone who wants to establish a 'win at all costs' or 'I'm on top of this issue in every way' image as part of personal ambition at the expense of team work. When you identify distraction in the workplace, it may be one element in punditry or more complicated office politics. It certainly isn't clear analytical thinking.

As well as substantial or side issues, a classic distraction tactic is to **highlight a trivial point**. In particular, this type of distraction focuses on a single small factual error or omission by an opponent. The unscrupulous operator then roasts them mercilessly for it. The conscious ploy is that by being seen to 'win' on this minor point, the proponent is perceived as winning the primary issue as well.

However, there are likely to be many facts and figures involved in presenting the usual complex business case or review. It is always possible that there will be some mistakes but the killer question is, "Are they critical facts which, if wrong, will bring down the whole proposal?"

In practice, one minor inaccuracy will not undermine the main proposal, reverse conclusions and redirect recommendations. This is the context which must be held at the forefront of the mind in assessing objections and queries when someone focuses on one fact among many.

It is also absolutely essential to ensure that any impression that a whole case has been discredited because of one figure is countered immediately. Point out that, despite the vigorous correction of that one fact, the original proposition is still supported by the factual evidence which stands.

It can also help sometimes to play the '**Since...How...**' game with such a diversionary attempt. Since x should really be y, how does the y value change all the other evidence offered? This brief and systematic exercise very quickly and clearly communicates to everyone present the insignificant degree of the correction. In such a circumstance, it is then practically impossible for the exponent of the tactic to return to it.

Not The Worst' or NTW is another form of distraction. This is the argument: x may be bad but y is even worse so why do anything about x? Any police officer patrolling the roads could become a millionaire if they were to be paid an extra day's salary every time they are told to stop harassing speeding drivers and 'catch real criminals'.

Welcome to one of the most popular usages of the 'NTW' argument. Essentially it says, "What I am doing is not bad because others are doing worse. "

We can see the interesting use of changing definition – the objector is someone who speeds but, despite breaking the traffic laws, does not classify themselves as a 'real' criminal – presumably they are thinking of burglars, robbers, rapists, murderers and so on. But logic dictates that if speeding is dangerous to other road users then why should it not be addressed in addition to all the other problems? The one does not exclude the other.

The response is to point out that both issues should be addressed while there may be issues of prioritisation, NTW needs to be countered. In business, this type of distraction has applications for monitoring and evaluation, presentations and verbal reports under pressure. It can turn up when annual budget lines are being determined for the next financial year or three year development plan.

NTW can occur uncomfortably in personal appraisals and target performance (especially within a close team context): "I didn't meet a couple of my objectives this year but others in the team have missed four or five. So why am I being hassled?"

NTW can therefore apply to corporate or personal performance with tarnished reputations and bonuses at stake. Always the message is, "However poorly I/the team/department/working group are performing, this is still acceptable because someone else is underachieving even more. "

10.4 Expectation

A political tactic also finds its way into monitoring and evaluation exercises, reviews and appraisals. This is 'expectation'. Essentially, when there is under-performance, poor results or difficult figures which run counter to desired trends, there is a standardised response to any challenge: "X was expected, anyway."

What such a response is trying to achieve is nothing constructive; rather, it is an attempt to minimise PR damage. This type of 'managed response' also serves to deflect criticism away from any responsibility or to save face in the light of strong evidence which contradicts the original planning.

According to the tactic, because the train crash is seen coming then it is somehow less destructive when it happens. That really doesn't make sense and the correct response consists of pointing out exactly that truth. The corollary is the matched question: "At what stage in the sequence of events preceding the poor outcome did that outcome become 'expected'? – Why was it evident?" It can be softened diplomatically and turned to constructive use by asking what can be learned by the team, working group or others from these answers.

10.5 Verbal comparison

It is possible to change an argument subtly by exaggerating a situation in a disguised manner. This can be achieved by using similes (It is like....) or a metaphor (word picture). The degree of difference or significance conveyed by the comparison or word picture, however, differs from the truth and can shift the argument into side issues. (A classic, popular example is when people compare some single poor-quality experience to the third world.)

You have to work through the comparison, show where it diverges from the situation you are actually facing and emphasise the impact of the true scenario. The response has to be clinical: "It is not like.....because it overstates [insert factor]. It is really like this...." and then repeat the actual status of the argument or assessment. In a sense, this formula is also an example of 'refusal of argument' (section 11).

Unfortunately, the misleading impact of a simile or metaphor can be increased further by using humour. The critical thinker risks putting themself at the usual disadvantage of appearing boring and pedantic they respond. One option therefore is to openly acknowledge the situation by saying: "That's a great comment but it doesn't really work for what we need. It exaggerates [insert factor] and that's not going to be funny when we see the results." Another effective response is to demonstrate that the false presentation method can lead to very different conclusions so that everyone needs to return to the facts and stick closely to them.

At this point it is necessary to have all the actual figures available for re-stating the assessment of the situation and correcting 'morphing'. It is even better if you can offer a like-with-like comparison but this needs to be carefully worked through. The match grid mentioned earlier in the book again is a useful tool at this juncture and in general it can be helpful to turn verbal comparisons into written studies as part of the response process. It allows clearer communication, unhurried reflection and a clear structuring of facts side stepped by a quick word picture.

10.6 Rubbishing the Witness

From time to time in reports of court cases you can read dramatic – indeed, sometimes lurid and unrestrained - accounts concerning the credibility or otherwise of witnesses. One side maintains that the witness has valuable information which they will declare openly and honestly under oath; the other side declaims known personal weaknesses or reveals past history which they insist will render the oath meaningless and make the witness unreliable for the purposes of the judicial process. But why is the witness going through their own trial within a trial?

The answer is a belief in the idea that you can rubbish the evidence if you rubbish the witness. You undermine the impact of the evidence you do not accept if you cast doubt on the wisdom of placing any trust in the person providing that evidence.

Despite its untruth, this belief extends to the dynamics of meetings and written reviews alike. Outright abuse and humiliation are illegal and subject to misconduct proceedings and employment tribunals. However, more subtle approaches may still do the job. Sweeping statements shared at the water cooler along the lines of "Arthur always takes a negative view of projects like this" are an alternative means of undermining confidence.

Ethics apart, such a generalisation should be rejected – firstly on the grounds that such an assertion is unproven even if there are some individual examples of Arthur's opposition to certain endeavours or proposals. Secondly, so what? Arthur may have made the right call anyway, past history not necessarily being the sole and absolute determinant of current accuracy. Last but not at all least, a conclusion has been implied without any consideration of the detail and data.

10.7 'Straw man'

Moving argument on to a debate about credibility rather than evidence can also be seen as a wilful example of the' straw man' technique. This is the well-known tactic of stating an opponent's position in a significantly misrepresentative way, thoroughly shredding the misrepresentation and thus leaving the impression that the original proposal or evidence has been successfully countered.

Although usually a calculated move, it can also be unintentional, driven by an outrage created by the listener simply misunderstanding key points. Whatever the motivation, the principle is the same: earliest possible correction explaining what is wrong and why, and re-stating the original view and summary evidence.

The best defence is to listen carefully when someone else is talking about what you are saying, as opposed to putting forward their own views or evidence. At the earliest opportunity, you must intervene in order to prevent the mistaken impression gaining strength around the meeting.

Section 11: Just Say NO

Refusal

In this final chapter we draw together a number of tactics to which the common response has to be, "I refuse to play that game". The proposer or presenter is making outrageous statements or limiting options so unrealistically that you have to do the mental equivalent of turning your back on them and walking away.

However, instead of keeping on walking in the opposite direction, a more constructive approach is to return bearing positive alternative suggestions, relevant facts and interpretations. You then state them so clearly and firmly that the original stance is set aside and the 'new' choices are explored.

You also have a great incentive in taking a proactive stance. Acquiescence is not an option as any lack of resistance morphs into actual agreement when everything is put on the record. At the very least, any later questioning as problems manifest themselves and cracks appear in the initiative comes across as pathetic whining and passing the buck. This is not the stuff of promotion and marketing credibility.

I readily acknowledge that contesting an assertion can require some diplomatic skill alongside the actual rational counter-presentation itself. Particularly in financially vulnerable times, you do not want to risk being the one labelled unjustly as 'not a team player'! And this holds doubly true when you have to take on an overbearing line manager, director, business partner or working group facilitator

This in turn relates to over-confidence (section 9) or punditry (section 7.5) with all that implies concerning underlying issues of self-esteem on the part of the proposer. However, let's at least deal with the main problem which falls within the remit of this book – false propositions, arguments and one-line conclusions which need stopping dead in their tracks.

11.1 False Dilemma

The first NO scenario to deal with is that of the 'false dilemma'. Here the manager, consultant or marketing/sales guru offers an' either/or' choice. That strict dichotomy alone may be over-simplistic and seriously misleading. So much in business, as in life generally, comes in the form of a continuous spectrum or a wide-ranging series of recognised variations.

Recently I was confronted with a colour card for all the paints available for purchase from our local DIY store. I was left hankering for the good old days when there was just straight red, blue, green, yellow and so on. Now whites routinely shade into creams and then into pinks, all with long, exotic or aspirational names which are a huge embarrassment to vocalise in public, even in the aforementioned DIY store. The point is that there are subtle and near-continuous variations and while we can refer to the distinct colour of pink for convenience, this fails to fully reflect the actual availability of choice.

This point should be in the mind of anyone who hears a sale presentation or trend projection with recommended actions or expenditures using the statement formula: Option/outcome can only be A or non-A. If you know or can check outside the meeting to find that A actually has degrees of variation then this 'either or' argument is immediately a false one. It needs to be rejected firmly by pointing out that such a sharp distinction does not correspond with reality – give a list of the variations or describe the spectrum that A covers. The point can be reinforced by cataloguing – if time permits – the different consequences arising from each of the variations.

But it can be even more complicated because such a 'black and white' offering of two alternatives can have a calculated or even unpleasant subtext. And that masked but determined message will be something along the lines of: "Do it the right way [my way] and soar upwards to business heaven **or** do it any other way whatsoever and expect to plummet into business hell." Teamwork means everyone doing things one way only - no choice, no input.

The response is to raise alternatives either within the meeting itself or as quickly as possible afterwards, using the official communications routes that have already been agreed. This will help take personality out of the equation to some degree. Beyond that, there are specialist management books concerning handling difficult staff and you may therefore have some additional bedtime reading.....

A final word about neglected options: the critical thinker does have a natural ally in the business world and that is the 'creativity' management consultant. This specialist brings innovative thinking skills to bear so that staff are trained to look routinely beyond simplistic or manipulative 'either or' approaches to decision-making. This is also an effective long-term answer to the strong and common personal factors which feature in the 'false dilemma' which is why I'm delighted to include such a business in the resources section.

11.2 Illogical structure: re-stating the argument

This second 'Just say No' scenario deals with a wide range of arguments which break down because they have inbuilt fallacies. In critical thinking, a sound argument means that there are two elements:

- Logically correct form
- True premises give a true conclusion

There are faults in arguments and presentations which are hidden by the wordings and flow of explanation.

This means that a close scrutiny is needed in case there is a gap in the logic (as opposed to simply missing out stages of the thought process or assuming they are self-evident to the recipients). It also means that every premise has to stand as a provably true statement in its own right. The link between the premises and the final conclusion has to be direct and valid.

If we consider the need to verify the logic, first of all, then there is a need to cultivate detachment in the middle of sometimes pressurised meetings. Here, we move the focus on how we feel personally about ideas and whether we agree or not with the proposed conclusions to the structure of the presentation leading to those conclusions.

The first step is to reduce the many words and reasons to a series of key premises – simple sentences suffice, especially in the limited time that is usually available during meetings or sales pitches. Each key statement or premise is numbered and the evidence for each one can be clearly noted and examined. Then the logical links between premises in this skeletal form of the argument can also be observed and checked.

Additionally, it is vital to recognise that a conclusion may or may not be correct despite the premises which come before it. It would be far too easy – it *is* far too easy – for someone to point to a reasonable conclusion, sit back and say: "This is all logical." It is not.

The value of putting the argument into simple, numbered statements can allow us to see the accuracy and completeness of premises – the key arguments or assertions. It also allows us to determine if the conclusion clearly derives from the previous material and is reasonable.

This approach of reducing arguments to a skeleton form is something of an acquired skill, although it doesn't require any kind of a doctorate. The complexity and delivery style, number of words and nuances all conspire to hide the skeleton beneath. Persistence is worth it, not just for personal professional competence but also for explaining your analysis plainly to others.

For that is the key to a number of propositions and even detailed arguments: to re-state an illogical structure in a series of premises (it may be useful to note key evidence for each alongside) and show how they are valid or fail as described above. In this way, you can refuse to accept unjustified leaps in logic or false premises and reject the process. Instead of looking like a member of the 'awkward squad', however, by re-stating in simple terms, you are seen to demonstrate incisiveness and can gain necessary support for collective rejection of the original idea.

There are other instances in which re-stating the issue and process cut through calamitous illogicality and enable a clear rejection to be made – and understood by others. The first is that of the classic **circular argument**.

For example, are CEOs really in senior management just for their salaries and bonuses? Debater #1 contends they have a dedication to the strength of their companies. Debater #2 highlights several instances of high bonuses versus declining performance, declarable assets and stock market values. Debater #1 then responds either that 'true' or 'real' CEOs honourably refuse salary increases or bonuses when the companies are struggling. Note in this instance that the definition of a CEO in the mind of Debater #1 already presupposes the very viewpoint that was still waiting to be proved by review of the evidence.

Here, debater #2 can point out that the assumptions and points to be proved are the same.

Other forms of assuming what is to be proved or justified are rather less obvious than the circular argument, and more difficult to detect:

- Prejudicial language with emotional overtones. The issue is praised or damned before the final decision is actually made or other data is even assessed

- Building the conclusion or viewpoint into initial introductions or terms of reference

- Biased criteria when collecting data, a variation of the 'Not looking' bias (section 3). Basically, anything which does not fit the proposition is not searched for as energetically, or recorded as diligently, as the items being sought in line with the argument or hypothesis.

As mentioned earlier, the correct response is to point out the exact nature of the pre-loaded verdict and where it has occurred. Re-state what needs to be demonstrated and make sure definitions are agreed, understood and without built-in bias. Then move on to the factual evidence available.

11.3 Patronising

In some ways this is a corollary to the prestige-based deceits (section 9) as it can be based on a line manager – employee dynamic within a public setting. Actually, it verges on psychological bullying, taking advantage of hierarchical position and an audience to enact a calculated choice of cheap shot over real discussion. For this reason it becomes another situation where you just say no to the whole thing.

If the subordinate is arguing a position which does not find favour with the line manager, the latter waits until the statement is complete. They then respond with a comment along the lines of: "I don't understand exactly what you are saying here/how the evidence relates to your conclusions. You and your thinking are too sophisticated/advanced/etc for our needs here."

The tone of mockery, the implication that the argument is rubbish because otherwise how would a (superior) line manager fail to grasp the delivery, the knowledge around the room of the relative status of the two – all combine to achieve an effective put down. It is the intellectual equivalent of the guillotine. One merciless stroke, delivered sharply, kills off the argument in a very public way.

How do you oppose this metaphorical and potentially career-stalling beheading? Here, the refusal to play by the imposed and distasteful rules inflicted by the line manager comes in the form of pulling back so the blow proves ineffective. You 'concede' graciously – then attack with determination but in a measured way that is, in truth, every bit as calculated as the original put down.

In practical terms, you reply to the patronising verdict by saying something like: "I'm sorry that what I've said is unclear to you." You then continue with the offer: "Let me put it this way, instead...." Re-word and simplify premises and evidence, repeat and emphasise links, use additional visual aids like impromptu flow diagrams with a marker on a flipchart. In this way, you explain – and, vitally, are seen by everyone present to explain - everything so clearly and completely that the point is clearly made.

The line manager is at the very least side-lined by the re-worded argument, and with the original ploy now laid bare in front of the meeting. The personal aspect can also be reduced by maintaining regular eye contact with the entire room instead of staring back at the line manager. This tactic, as positive body language, also gains good will to reinforce the application of the analytical response and, hopefully, win the day.

11.4 Forcing answers

Basically, the idea is to pressure you into answers which severely weaken your project plan, case presentation, tender or sales pitch. The tactic relies upon two interdependent elements:

- Aggressive, haranguing quick-fire questioning (usually with body language to match)
- A question which is worded in such a way as to dictate the response

Let's deal with the second element before returning to the manner in which the tactic is delivered. The actual structure of the prejudiced question can come in one of three general forms. The first version is the simplest: "Surely, you agree with the principles of x?" or, "Obviously, you wouldn't go against the values of y, would you?"

The signpost language of words like 'Surely' is a warning that there something less than neutral about to come. (Even more so when a phrase like, 'Do you admit...?' is deployed, especially as the word 'admit' has overtones of guilt or of shiftiness.)

The response is to refuse to admit a simple yes or no, and answer the question exactly as you wish. It is also a fair tactic to point out how the phrasing of the question presupposes a particular answer – and add that you want to give the right and *truthful* response instead. The very last word is important as it emphasises the gap between what the questioner wants and what the full and honest answer should be.

A second type of 'forcing answers' involves **bundling** two or more separate issues/questions into a single, highly complicated, question with a demand for a single answer. This one answer is taken to be a response for all the elements that were included.

"Do you admit that your company prioritisations policy has led to breaches of expenditure ceilings, less efficient record-keeping, poor ICT investment, increased complaints over product quality and plummeting staff morale? Yes or No?"

Again, and for all the advantages just stated for the response to the second question type, it is best to refuse to play the game and answer with a one-word umbrella answer. Respond by saying, "That is several questions – one answer for all of them is **obviously** ridiculous." The highlighted word adds emphasis and challenges the questioner to be much more reasonable and rational, all in front of others. It deals with any intentional 'grandstanding' immediately and decisively.

Then it becomes possible to break down the multiple issues into separate questions with individual answers. To be most emphatic in the response, follow the sequence of Q1 + A1, Q2 + A2, Q3 + A3.

All the steps needed to mount an effective response seem so straightforward that they immediately raise the question, "If it is so easy then why does it need to be spelt out?" The explanation lies with the first element mentioned at the beginning of the discussion about forcing answers. The questions are not posed in a measured way with a chance for cautious consideration; they are delivered in rapid-fire style, quite possibly with a degree of raw and inflammatory emotion.

The manner of delivery creates a psychological intimidation which works effectively alongside the questions themselves. A defence against this psychological aspect of forcing answers is the '**Stranger In The Street**' concept. Think to yourself, "Would a stranger that I just met in the street talk to me like this?" The context and answer to this not unreasonable question gives confidence and a constructive sense of injustice. Such attitudes counter the intended intimidation and, most importantly, facilitate exactly that frame of mind which refuses become a victim of forced admissions.

11.5 Dictating the answer

This form of argument process is most definitely unsubtle and the heading gathers together a number of tactics. We have seen some of them earlier in this handbook but in all cases there is now an additional extreme element of pressure to the action. It is much more pronounced or militant than 'forcing answers' although arguably belonging to the very end of a common spectrum of such behaviour.

The forcefulness will certainly be expressed verbally through the deliberate choice of vocabulary (emotional, scornful, sarcastic, possibly swearing and certainly highly directional). It is backed up by 'aggressive' body language like jabbing the forefinger, wide arm sweeps, leaning forward and/or maintaining unbroken eye contact for longer than is usually the case in normal conversation.   The tone will be 'heavy' bass with slowed, purposeful delivery (section 9). The 'dictatorship' is heavily associated with punditry (section 7) but can come from any direction whenever managers, entrepreneurs and project teams are under pressure.

The most common forms of 'dictating the answer' can be summarised and countered along the following lines:

1. **Framing (section 5) on steroids!** Terms like' surely' and 'obviously' are routinely included but

here the ante is definitely upped. Phrases like: "You must see that....", "This can only mean..." are also warning signs to the listeners that further questions, however appropriate, are just not welcome. Conclusions feature imperatives like 'We need to......now' and refer to a single line of action or just a couple of variants.

Remove the personal aspect by taking out all such phrases, and use neutral vocabulary to restate the single option that is offered and then add alternative options. These can be immediately realistic and practical, or theoretical pending further evidence or research.

2. **Avalanching**: A catch-all term like, "For all sorts of reasons" takes recipients directly to conclusions or recommendations, by-passing many (and possibly all the most critical) elements of data and analysis. Like an avalanche, a single unbreakable 'mass' statement simply sweeps all before it in one movement.

As elsewhere, the proper response should be an insistence on seeing a list of all those reasons. If you have a sense of irony or mischief you can argue back, "For all sorts of reasons we need to see a list of the reasons!"

The next practical step is, working from such a list, to carry out a series of individual analyses. This is where opportunities, additional costs, risk management inadequacies or logistics points all turn up. It is a constructive approach which also enables you to nail your opponent's underpants to the mast – with the proposer still wearing them!

Avalanching may be more likely to be experienced at middle/low management levels as a dissection process occurs more automatically at senior management team and board level in company hierarchies. With all the psychological pressure and unpleasantness which surrounds any attempts to challenge instances of 'dictating the answer' it is difficult to stay the course. The Stranger In The Street mental firmness is helpful in these more extreme circumstances.

However you find yourself motivated to fight back, the effort is worth it. After all, consider what might happen if the original plans and presentations are left to pass unchallenged. The unsubstantiated final assertion may well find its way into the recommendations and options which inform company strategy – and it will then be your job to make the impossible work out profitably......

3. **Inappropriate analogies** (section 10). The presenter or speaker morphs into a fully-fledged,

rabble-rousing orator with spittle at the corners of their mouth. Analogies are extremely colourful and vivid even if they lack logical credibility or fail to reflect the actual situation.

The response here is a gracious, "Without getting pedantic, that analogy doesn't apply because the situation looks like..." or "We need to keep a clear view of the real problem which is....." The re-stating which you apply should be used as the baseline for all further discussion. The proposer may keep on trying to return to their suppositions and exaggerating analogies so you have to be prepared to keep on referring to the re-stated version of the issue as many times as proves necessary.

4. **'One-swipe demolition'.** This usually occurs after some initial summaries of figures, monitoring and evaluation or other project/SMART assessment. Rather than an objective consideration of all presented data and aspects – good and bad – there is a sweeping, angry one line criticism of the whole issue. There is no discrimination or discretion between factors and roles whatsoever. It descends on the meeting agenda and attendees with all the delicacy of a wrecking ball in mid-swing.

This differs from avalanching because demolition is a reply to a proposal and not an assertion. However, a defence similar to that for avalanching is appropriate here.

5. **Brush aside**. I once had an in-depth conversation with a leading politician who talked me through some of their basic responses to hostile journalists. One technique was the 'brush aside' for those occasions when a journalist said something along the lines of, "This policy hasn't worked – you're not seeing good results. Surely this is a total disaster?" The comeback would be forthright and immediate: "No, I don't see it like that at all. I see it like this [insert viewpoint] because of facts/reasons A, B and C".

The 'brush aside' is concise, structured and decisive – an excellent addition to the critical thinking emergency response kit. The structural aspect is important because it gives other meeting participants and stakeholders identified starting points to discuss, and therefore facilitates positive development. The decisiveness provides a means of stopping the rant and letting others contribute, and conciseness is a statement in itself of your alternative leadership in the room or wider process. It removes focus from just that one person with the negative and destructive attitude and gives a chance to move on with the actual purpose of the gathering or shared communication.

In all five instances just described, the counter points are not simply verbal. Body language should not just be non-threatening but obviously open (arms forward, brief eye contact with all in the room, sitting up rather than forward, small hand gestures with open palms, relaxed facial expression). Tone should be warm but otherwise neutral to match a non-emotional vocabulary.

It also helps to remember that often 'dictating the answer' is a displacement response to the accumulating weight of background pressures bearing down on the proposer. They are desperate in turn to achieve a decisive resolution or result to ease that pressure and are trying to force the pace or outcome accordingly. 'Dictating the answer' is not usually a personal attack. You may have to repeat this under your breath several times as a mantra but that is not a bad thing in itself. It also allows a few moments to choose your next critical thinking tool to apply to the situation or information under consideration.

11.6 Artificial loading

The cost or difficulty of a project or case is overstated by introducing features which may not actually have been planned by opponents or proven necessary to fulfilling aims and objectives. It may be possible to direct decision-makers towards one option by inflating the costs of all the alternatives to make them look uncompetitive and relatively complex undertakings. This can apply to capital engineering projects which are subject to political debate and inquiries.

Some of the political arguments during the 2011 referendum about adopting the Alternative Vote (AV) system in place of the existing First Past The Post process (FPTP) for UK elections fell into this category. There was debate not just over the cost of £250 million for bringing in AV but also some suggestion of an additional £130 million requirement for electronic counting machines. But such machines were not a necessary requirement for AV: ballot papers could be counted exactly like they had been hitherto for the existing FTFP, and any ballot system could be supported by such machines. In effect, anyone raising the issue of the counting machines was inflating the apparent costs, giving an illogical, invalid reason for rejecting AV.

A practical response constitutes a clear refusal to accept the artificial loading:

> (1) Highlight each 'loaded' feature as a significant inaccuracy and baseless assertion

(2) Repeat the original argument, planning and aims/objectives

(3) Emphasise the logical, original recommendations or costs of client's planning/intention

(4) Conclude with a contrast between the misrepresentation and the actual cost

And now, the blindfold falls away – congratulations! You are able to function more effectively and decisively without the former restrictions, hesitations and unjustified confidence. There is one final thought: without your blindfold you can now see how many others still have theirs, and how they are left blundering around. The fact that they are trying to do this with purposeful intent does not lessen the pain and bruising as they walk unswervingly into substantial obstacles lying in the path of the unknowing. Help others in your business to realise they can improve their critical abilities and profit-making performance too. Check out the end pieces to see how CTCP can loosen the knot and lift the blindfold for your colleagues and contacts.

Section 12: Sources, Resources and Further Reading

On-line source for business sector critical thinking:

www.agilecriticalthinking.com
Clear Thinking Clear Profit is the official
European affiliate of American business
Agile Critical Thinking
(Anne and Charlie Kreitzberg)

On-line sources for general critical thinking:

1. www.lawgazette.co.uk/in-practice/practice-points/pitfalls-of-percentages

2. http://critical-thinkers.com

3. www.thegreatcourses.com   (Argumentation and Critical Thinking)

4. www.en.wikipedia.org/wiki/Critical_thinking and related articles with full citations

5. www.bbc.co.uk   (Michael Blastland: Go Figure series)

6. www.learningdevelopment.plymouth.ac.uk University of Plymouth (2010), Study   Guide 8: 'Critical Thinking', Learning Development

7. www.royalinstitutephilosophy.org/think/index

8. www.straightstatistics.org

9. Thouless, Robert H. (1953), *Straight and Crooked Thinking*. London: Pan Books Ltd. http://en.wikipedia.org/wiki/Robert_H._Thouless PDF download

Related fields:
1. www.thecreativethinkingcompany.co.uk (Prith Biant)

2. www.mikepagan.com Presentations and self-management skills (Mike Pagan)

3. www.sellingandpersuasiontechniques.com/nonverbal-communication.html

4. www.topwsisolutions.co.uk_ Internet marketing (Bal Butter)

5. www.karmanetworking.co.uk_ Networking, events and training (Tej Jhite)

Blastland, M and Dilnot, A. (2007), *The Tiger that Isn't - Seeing Through a World of Numbers*. London: Profile Books Ltd
Berlin, Isaiah (1997) *The Proper Study of Mankind*, London: Chatto and Windus, (Random House)

Cottrell, S. (2005), *Critical thinking skills.* Basingstoke: Palgrave Macmillan

Hutton, R. and Hutton, G. (2008) *Passing Oxbridge Admissions Tests.* Exeter: Learning Matters Ltd (www.learningmatters.co.uk)

Kida, Thomas E. (2006), *Don't believe everything you think: the 6 basic mistakes we make in thinking*, Amherst, New York: Prometheus Books

Tetlock, Philip E. (2005), *Expert Political Judgment: How Good Is It? How Can We Know?*, Princeton, N.J.: Princeton University Press, pp. 125–128

Van den Brink-Budgen, R. (2000) *Critical Thinking for Students.* Oxford: How To Books

Wallace, M and Wray, A (2011), *Critical Reading and Writing for Postgraduates* (Second edition), London: Sage Publications Ltd

LinkedIn Groups:
1. Pearson – Critical Thinking in the Workplace

2. Problem Solving through Critical and Creative Thinking

Section Index

Section	Issues
1: Critical thinking	1.1 Definition 1.2 Organisational importance 1.3 Commercial 'pain' 1.4 Competitive advantages 1.5 Making CT work for you
2: Foundations	2.1 Components of critical thinking 2.2 Self-questioning and clarity 2.3 Common assumptions 2.4 Situational assumptions 2.5 The QEP triangle
3: Context deficiency	3.1 Incomplete data 3.2 Omission 3.3 Confirmation bias 3.4 Primacy effect 3.5 Over-simplification 3.6 Quantitative vagueness 3.7 Not looking
4: Percentages	4.1 Percentages only 4.2 Percentage breakdown (sets) - visuals 4.3 Percentages versus absolute numbers 4.4 Editorialising 4.5 Like-with-like (match grid) 4.6 Percentages and context deficiency
5: Overviews	5.1 Averages 5.2 Trends 5.3 Sampling and surveys 5.4 Information visualisation 5.5 Framing 5.6 Batching 5.7 Ratio bias 5.8 Compromise

6: Correlation	6.1 Cause
	6.2 Correlation links - parallel and chain
	6.3 Obscurity
	6.4 Complexity
7: Exaggeration and guesswork	7.1 Headlining
	7.2 Perception versus calculation
	7.3 Relative frequency
	7.4 Speculation
	7.5 Punditry
	7.6 Plural numbers
8: Emotions	8.1 Overtones
	8.2 Personal subjectivity
	8.3 Softening up
	8.4 Anger
	8.5 Prejudice
	8.6 Sound bites and slogans
9: Non-verbal and status arguments	9.1 Positive image projection
	9.2 Prestige
	9.3 Repetition
10: Changing the argument	10.1 Toning down
	10.2 Changing definition
	10.3 Distraction
	10.4 Expectation
	10.5 Verbal comparison
	10.6 Rubbishing the witness
	10.7 Straw man
11: Refusal	11.1 False dilemma
	11.2 Re-stating the argument
	11.3 Patronising
	11.4 Forcing answers
	11.5 Dictating the answer
	11.6 Artificial loading

CTCP Workshop Programmes

Do you want to make more profit?

Avoid decisions which waste money, time and effort

Reduce inefficiency and expenditure

Improve sales presentations, tenders, evaluation reports, expert evidence and strategic reviews

Increase income and client diversification

Impress customers with professionalism and service delivery

Retain clients and add new ones – even during difficult times

CTCP can equip you to do this in as little as four hours – and that includes lunch time!

PARAMOUNT *PROGRAMME for:*

Senior management teams – directors/heads of departments

Board members (including voluntary sector trustees)

Emerging leaders

Bespoke programme delivered in 1-to-1 or small group sessions (3 – 8 participants)
Core objectives: review and reinforce CT skills systematically; understand CT skills as company-wide management tool; develop strategic role free from micromanagement burdens

THINK! *PROGRAMME for:*

HR and marketing personnel
Development and project managers
Company fast-track programme participants and supervisors
Middle/junior managers in place or under super-vision
Management consultants and trainers
Business Studies students and lecturers
Journalists and journalism students
Academics managing collaborative projects with commercial organisations

Bespoke programme delivered in workshop, seminar or lecture delivery formats appropriate to client needs (4+ participants). Select from pre-prepared modules or order tailor-made units according to specific requirements.

Core objectives: introduce systematic CT skills; understand CT skills as tool for customer relations and line management communications; apply CT skills with immediate effect to current operational role(s)

For a no obligation discussion about your business needs and programme contents, and how to book, contact info@clearthinkingclearprofit.com or 07985 64 11 99

Clear Thinking Clear Profit supports the Midlands Air Ambulance

Please donate at www.midlandsairambulance.com

About the Author

Alan Wood wants to help people profit from their hard work by using critical thinking. He trained in the sciences and has since spent over thirty years in management, staff and volunteer training positions. He was Head of Medical Laboratory Services at two reference hospitals and a successful fundraising, region and major projects manager with competitive 'top 300' UK and overseas development agencies. He remains a volunteer emergency relief specialist in Information and Logistics, and worked among refugees in the DR Congo war zone. He also served in Haiti's immediate post-earthquake operations. He is a qualified Adult Education lecturer with both domestic and international management training experience.

Alan's passion is high quality analysis and decision-making – the motivation for writing this book and professional magazine articles, delivering his workshops, providing consultancy support and writing his blog: "Understanding Our Numbers-Driven World": www.alanwoodsblog.wordpress.com

Outside of work Alan is a keen hiker and runner which helps offset his love of chocolate. He enjoys reading modern novels and travel books.

Footnotes

[i] Kreitzberg, AP and Kreitzberg, C (2010). *The Business Case for Critical Thinking Skills*. Adapted from: http://www.agilecriticalthinking.com August 2011.

[ii] Adapted and expanded from: Hutton, R. and Hutton, G. (2008) *Passing Oxbridge Admissions Tests*. Chapter 3: Thinking Skills Assessment, Section 12, 'Critical Thinking', pages 23-25 and Chapter 5: TSA Writing Task, Section 21, 'Critical Thinking', pages 140-141. Learning Matters, Exeter, UK.

[iii] Adapted and expanded from: Zarefsky, David. "Underlying Assumptions of Argumentation." Argumentation: The Study of Effective Reasoning. DVD. Chantilly, VA: The Great Courses, 2006.

[iv] Adapted and expanded from: Hutton, R. and Hutton, G. (2008) *Passing Oxbridge Admissions Tests*. Chapter 3: Thinking Skills Assessment, Section 3, 'Identifying an assumption', pages 28-29. Learning Matters, Exeter, UK
[v] Connor, S (26 May 2011) http://www.independent.co.uk/travel/news-and-advice/the-real-danger-to-air-passengers-is-not-the-ash-cloud-andash-its-these-men-2289097.html

[vi] Connor, S – ditto, comments section associated with article

[vii] www.alcoholconcern.org.uk/news-centre/press-releases/off-licence-density-linked-to-alcohol-harm-in-under-18s (Sept 2011).

[viii] http://www.dailymail.co.uk/news/article-2033796/Give-birth-March-pilot-August-bricklayer-December-dentist-.html

[ix] Ditto